月河的流水 Remembrance of the Moon River

by Sheng-yen Lu

Translated by Nora Wang

A US Daden Culture Publication

US Daden Culture LLC
3440 Foothill Blvd.
Oakland, CA 94601
U.S.A.
Website: www.usdaden.com
Email: us.daden.culture@gmail.com

© 2013 by Sheng-yen Lu

The right of Living Buddha Lian-sheng, Sheng-yen Lu to be identified as author of this work including all translations based on his original writings, has been asserted by him in accordance with the Copyright, Designs, and Patents Act 1988.

All rights reserved. No part of this book may be reproduced in any form or by any means, electronic or mechanical, including photography, recording, or by any information storage or retrieval system or technologies now known or later developed, without permission in writing from the publisher.

Lu, Sheng-yen, 1945-
Remembrance of the Moon River/by Sheng-yen Lu;
translated by Nora Wang;
edited by Joanie Nguyen and Janny Chow;
proofread by Renee Cordsen.

Library of Congress Control Number (PCN): 2013939140
ISBN-13: 978-0-9858080-6-8
ISBN-10: 0985808063
1. True Buddha School. 2. Chinese-Tantrayana Buddhism.
Cover design and layout by US Daden Culture Design Team
Photograph by US Daden Culture
Set in Minion Pro 12
US Daden books are printed on acid-free paper and meet the guidelines for the permanence and durability set by the Council of Library Resources.

Printed in the U.S.A.

Special Acknowledgements

The True Buddha Translation Teams (TBTTs) would like to express the highest honor and deepest gratitude to Living Buddha Lian-sheng Sheng-yen Lu and Master Lianxiang for their continuing support and guidance on the translation effort. Without their compassion, wisdom, blessings, and encouragement, this project would not have reached fruition.

In addition, we would like to acknowledge the diligent work put forth by the following volunteers on this project: Nora Wang (translator), Joanie Nguyen (editor), Janny Chow (editor and quality control), and Renee Cordsen (proofreader and desk-top publication). We would like to thank these dedicated and selfless volunteers who have contributed their time and effort to promote the works of Living Buddha Lian-sheng, and to support the publications of US Daden Culture.

We would also like to extend our sincere appreciation to all other volunteers who work behind the scenes, facilitating the translation process, and handling administrative responsibilities.

May all volunteers be blessed with immeasurable merits. May all sentient beings benefit from the ocean of wisdom.

Table of Contents

1. I Want to Tell You About the Moon River — 1
2. Written for GaiGai — 5
3. Thoughts, Thoughts, Thoughts, Thoughts, Thoughts — 9
4. A Few Words About *The Rain Collection* — 13
5. Do You Understand the Emptiness of Cause and Effect? — 17
6. Standing in the Opposite Corner — 21
7. The Indelible Image of a Beautiful Lady — 25
8. The Lights Outside the Window — 29
9. The Game of Seesaw — 33
10. The Three Turnings of the Dharma Wheel — 37
11. Discovery of the Steely Glint — 41
12. Flying in Space — 45
13. Let Us Happily Recite the Mantra — 49
14. The Stars on the Ground — 53
15. I Live for You — 57
16. The Sadhana of Kurukulle — 61
17. Where Are You Hiding? — 65
18. The Tears in Your Eyes — 69

19. Never Thought of Temperature	73
20. The Light at the Moon River	77
21. Singing Flowers	81
22. The Opening of the Dragon King Shrine	85
23. The Height of Heavenly Beings	89
24. Flying Fish	93
25. You Are a Precious Rare Gem	97
26. It Happened to You	101
27. Liking Everyone	105
28. The Feeling of Being Misunderstood	109
29. Charming of the Five Blessings	113
30. Smiling Voices	117
31. Good Times Never Last	121
32. Charming Smile	125
33. Purely Fictional	129
34. Secret of Secrets	133
35. Sincere Gratitude	137
36. Let's Fly up to the Sky	141
37. Pay Respect to My Father	145
38. Even Misunderstandings Do Not Remain	149
39. Self Imposed Restrictions	153
40. Is GaiGai the White Dakini?	157

41. A Letter from President Obama	161
42. Disciples are Also Like Water	165
43. Self Authenticated Buddha-nature	169
44. The Feeling of Confusion	173
45. As an Illusion or As a Dream	177
46. Surpass Obstacles After Obstacles	181
47. Dharma Talks About the Sixth Patriarch	185
48. Self Disappearance	189
49. Hurry to Lishan [Pear Mountain]	193
50. Listening at the Wuling Farm	197
Appendix: A Gift of Wisdom (A Response from a Reader)	201
Glossary	211

1. I Want to Tell You About the Moon River

Many, many eons of lifetimes ago we lived at a place called the "Moon River." Where is this "Moon River"? I can only point to the sky, because the "Moon River" is one of the scenic sites in heaven by the "River of Heaven."

We used to be at the "Moon River," but we liked to roam. We liked to roam because we were not satisfied with the present. This is why you and I drifted along like the "roaming water." Roaming water has no home. It can only flow along through fate and destiny.

So we roamed on and on.

I remember that I was once a majestic "king" and you were the majestic "queen."

> The "Moon River" is full of fragrance.
> The "Moon River" has plenty of flowers.
> The "Moon River" is fortunately blessed.
> The "Moon River" is free from troubles and worries.

Our virtuous hearts were at peace. Our lives were in perfect beauty.

We had everything. I said it then that I will always take care of you and treat you nicely.

It is obvious that we had spent a long time together as if time stood still, like frozen in space. So you said, "We have to go forward and have a different life."

I asked, "What type of life?"

You answered, "Just a different kind of life."

I asked, "Isn't the present one good enough?"

You answered, "Perfect, but too perfect."

I asked, "Do you want to leave for a walk?"

You answered, "Yes."

So, I said, "Then let me be your guardian, for I am the only one who cares for you."

You answered, "Yes."

This is our eternal love that we promised to each other a long, long time ago. In today's terms, it is our vow.

I have come to understand that there is no standard of measurement for being blessed. One does not always realize one is blessed. Even if there is a standard, the measurement would be ambiguous.

Finally, our walk took us through many lives of reincarnations.

So, I put on the shoes of reincarnation and you also put on the shoes of reincarnation.

Once the shoes of reincarnation were on, they could not be removed. The shoes must keep on walking no matter how tired one gets.

I know you have been unjustly treated.

This is why I want to treat you well.

You used to be from heaven and had expectations of perfections, but you received none and thus became disappointed and distraught.

So, I appeared at this moment.

Will you let me stay and take care of you? Give you a little warmth when coldness surrounds you?

But to no avail.

I know very well.

If I could give you some care and attention, you will be able to emit exuberant fragrance with remarkable attractions that could never be forgotten.

This must be the result of our promise.

Poem: *Roaming*

> *Since leaving the "Moon River"*
> *Our memory faded*
> *When we meet again*
> *It will be the beginning*
> *Of another performance*
>
> *Flashing of affinity*
> *Is the magnetism*
> *Deeply attracting our souls*
> *Are the vows at the "Moon River"*
> *This is the meaning of a promise*

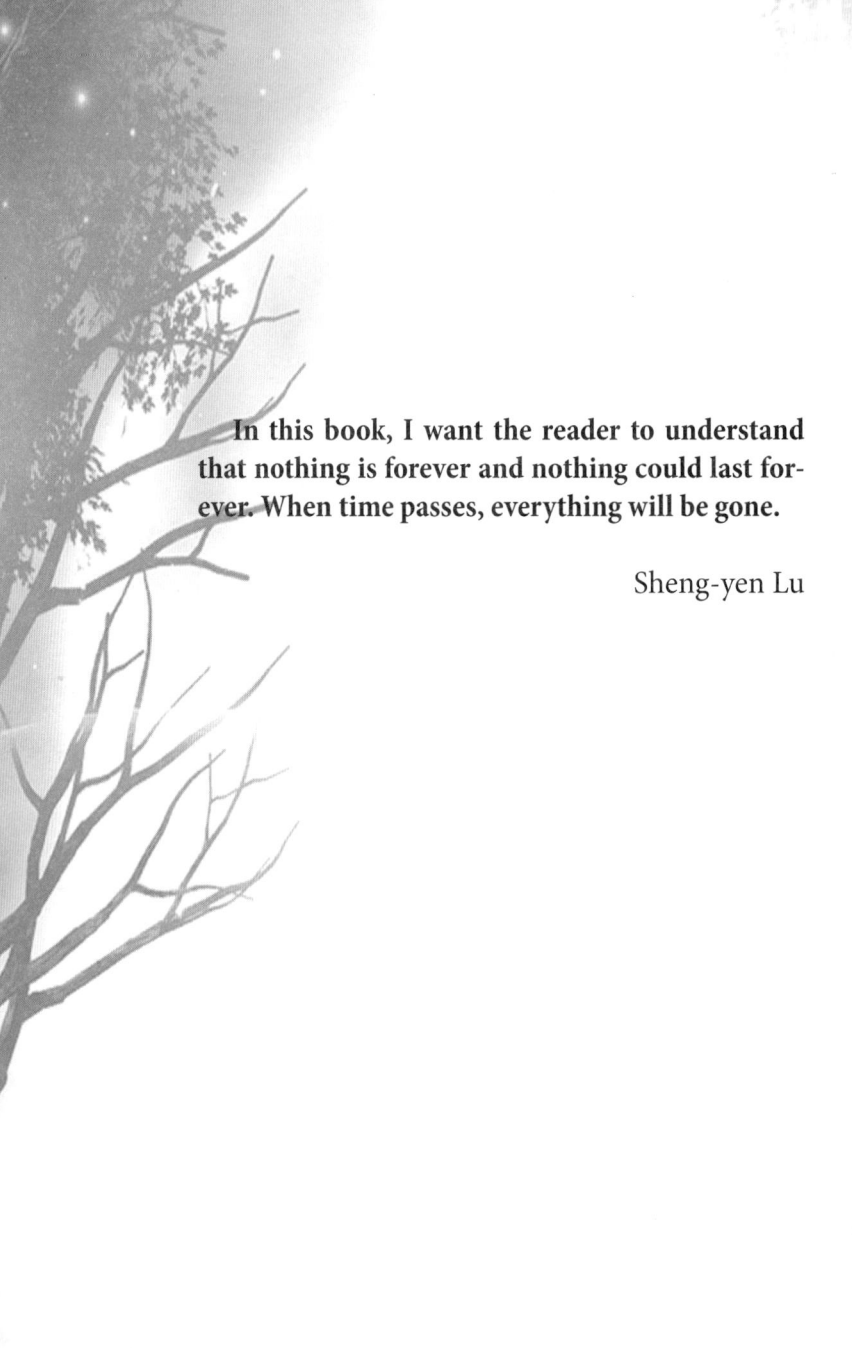

In this book, I want the reader to understand that nothing is forever and nothing could last forever. When time passes, everything will be gone.

Sheng-yen Lu

2. Written for GaiGai

After reading the first article, many of you may be puzzled. What is Grand Master Lu really writing about? Who is the "you" in this book?

I say, "Let it be about the heaven and earth!"

There is no preface in this book because the Moon River is timeless. Its existence has no beginning and no end. Therefore, a "preface" is not necessary.

The Moon River is in heaven.

I was once the King of the Moon River.

The "you" in this book could be the Queen of Moon River. "You" could also be the celestial ladies of Moon River or all of the celestial beings of Moon River.

It was not written about, to, or for any particular person. GaiGai is only a name I made up for name sake.

This book is a record of all my heart to heart talks between GaiGai and I.

Does Grand Master Lu have passion like the rest of us?

My answer is yes, no doubt about it - a hundred percent yes.

In this book, I want the reader to understand that nothing is forever and nothing could last forever. When time passes, everything will be gone.

I have mine.

GaiGai has GaiGai's.

In every life, GaiGai and I will be together, but our memories will be swept away like waves sweeping away imprints on the sand. Then calm is restored.

Do you all feel that in the end, life is truly empty?

Times of our suffering together.

Times of our laughter together.

Times of our disappointments together.

All of our togetherness.

From sadness to happiness and from parting to assembling.

Dissipating like smoke. Dissipating, dissipating, dissipating....

And then finally returning to emptiness.

This is why I am reserved from time to time.

***

GaiGai!

Don't you know that you are from the heaven's scenic site, the Moon River?

We made vows. You are perplexed because you simply can't remember.

But even so, the magnetism of our bodies continues to attract each other just like before.

We can lose ourselves in happiness, but the happiness of this world never lasts because disappointment always follows.

GaiGai!

We are incapacitated. We are unable to do anything about it. We have lost control.

All we can do is to wait....wait it out....
What are we waiting for? Nobody knows.
Ha! Ha!

Poem: *Waiting*

> *I lost my soul*
> *You said*
> *You already lost your soul*
> *GaiGai*
> *We have enjoyed this world*
> *Oh*
> *We followed our will*
> *For this feeling*
> *We don't know what will follow*

I think about how to realize my dream of delivering more sentient beings. I think about how to become a buddha and my wish that everyone becomes a buddha too.

Sheng-yen Lu

3. Thoughts, Thoughts, Thoughts, Thoughts, Thoughts

GaiGai! I will miss you! Each time I told you, you said, "I will miss you too."

In truth, my mind is full of thoughts. Sometimes I daydream, other times I reminisce and some thoughts are just mindless. Threads of thoughts keep pouring in like the rain.

I think that having hopes is a kind of blessing.

I have three types of thoughts:

    My faith.
    My hopes.
    My love.

I think about my principal deity, my Moon River and my root lineage - Vairocana Tathagata.

I think about how to realize my dream of delivering more sentient beings. I think about how to become a buddha and my wish that everyone becomes a buddha too.

And then there is my love.

A little bit of love for GaiGai. This little bit of love for GaiGai is so minute, but it gives me the most satisfaction.

We blend into one at the Moon River, so in this human world we also blend into one. Therefore, thinking of each other is necessary. Without these thoughts of you, the flower in my heart will wither.

We are not made of stone. We are not made of sand. We certainly are not made of steel or iron ore.

We are fortunate that we have the same faith, same hopes and the same love.

Frankly, there is nobody in my life. Every day the sun shines and the trees sway in the breeze, yet I pass each of those days by myself in loneliness.

Are there people around?

Yes.

Are your disciples around?

Yes.

Are there strangers around?

Yes.

Yet, I am still lonely because I am missing my heart, for my heart is with you.

***

I am dreaming again....

I want to take you to a far away country in Africa where no one knows us.

I want to take you to the Caribbean where we can feel the sea breeze underneath the palm trees.

I want to take you to a city in the Middle East desert, wearing turbans and experience an exotic way of life.

We could go to the North Pole or to the South Pole.

Fortunately, a special happiness comes from dreaming this way. Although these thoughts are empty, imaginary and unreal, it brings happiness to us both.

GaiGai!

Have you ever thought about returning to the Moon River? We miss the taste of the dew drops at the Moon River. We miss the clothing, the palace, and the astral travel of the Moon River.

I was the King.

You were the Queen.

I was the Prince.

You were the Princess.

We looked into each other's eyes and the smiles brought us unreserved happiness.

I wish you and my disciples would practice the Ten Virtuous Deeds. This way, we will all be able to return to the Moon River.

GaiGai!

Have you ever thought about the Moon River? Do you miss our Moon River?

This is the same joy as the bliss of "Vajra Play" in Vajrayana. I think this is the same as the Pureland of Ultimate Bliss.

Sheng-yen Lu

4. A Few Words About *The Rain Collection*

After the publication of the book *The Rain Collection*, people began to question if the "rain" really is just rain, or if it is a metaphor for something or someone?

Is it rain?

Is it someone?

Is it about someone who is related to "rain"?

The Rain Collection is a collection of sentimental, poetic short essays.

Many people commented on its exquisiteness, noting its similarities to young people's dreams. Ambassador Liao Dongzhou stationed in Seattle made several compliments, stating:

    Beautiful phrases,

    Delicate emotions,

    In-depth meanings,

    It is a unique book.

People asked me, "Who is the 'rain' in this book?"

I smiled, but did not answer.

They asked again.

I said, "It is the remembrance of my heart."

I can not reveal its meaning. You will have to keep guessing. The answer will never be revealed.

This book *Remembrance of the Moon River* is written for GaiGai. In many ways GaiGai could be an actual person, but could also be an imaginary person.

Is this book about a real person and real events or is it a fantasy and imaginary?

Let it continue to be a mystery.

I do not want to expose GaiGai because it is my deepest secret.

If GaiGai is ever revealed, both GaiGai and I will be sweating profusely, which is why GaiGai must remain an imaginary person.

***

At the Moon River:
    We were always happy.
    We had feelings of eternity.
    We had no hindrances or troubles.
    We could do whatever our hearts desired.
    We understood everything, and everything was clear.

We could not be held back by time, for it is timeless at the Moon River, which is inconceivable by people on earth.

I will never change.

GaiGai will never change.

Moon River is a profound world.

GaiGai!

Do you know that the rain at Moon River sparkles? Sparkling everywhere. The sparkles are soft, colorful and dazzling.

The rain at the Moon River surrounds us, flashing and quivering indescribably.

After surrounding us, the rain wraps around us, very tightly at first and then loosely. Finally, our bodies became one and our hearts united.

Suspended in yoga for a long, long time. This is the same joy as the bliss of "Vajra Play" in Vajrayana. I think this is the same as the Pureland of Ultimate Bliss. GaiGai thinks so too. We were just very, very happy.

Poem:

> *The raindrops of the Moon River*
> *Were like the musical notes of light*
> *Bonded momentarily in the eternal bliss*
> *Filled with utmost joyfulness that contained*
> *Both sounds of laughter and crying*

Sometimes you can't help but feel disappointed, for nothing stays the same forever. Sooner or later, love, friendship, and family ties will turn into emptiness.

Sheng-yen Lu

5. Do You Understand the Emptiness of Cause and Effect?

GaiGai! From what I know, Buddhism teaches:
Impermanence - nothing is forever, and therefore empty.
Cause & effect is empty - when the cause is gone, the effect is erased as well.
Eighteen Fields - six senses, six sense organs, & six sense consciousness are empty.
The ultimate reality is empty - Buddha-nature is the absolute truth.

Sometimes you can't help but feel disappointed, for nothing stays the same forever. Sooner or later, love, friendship, and family ties will turn into emptiness.

When impermanence arrives, emotional ties end.
Partings begin when cause and effect ceases.
The loss of Eighteen Fields is when things return to ashes.
GaiGai, my experiences with my disciples have been enlightening.
My concern for their well being was reciprocated with abusiveness towards me. My sincerity was repaid by desertion. I gave him extra

empowerments and blessings, but instead he insulted me and slandered and defamed me.

I was warm to him, yet he responded with coldness.

I gave him my love, yet he reciprocated with hate.

I gave him purity, yet he returned with filth.

I understand impermanence, emptiness of cause and effect, emptiness of the Eighteen Fields, and emptiness of the ultimate reality and because of this I was able to let go and not take it personally.

GaiGai!

You should know that at Moon River there are no walls, real or imaginary. Everything is crystal clear.

We were crystal clear celestial beings.

No one in this world has been to Moon River, therefore, they can only use their imagination.

Celestial beings all have pure white hearts. There are no black, gray, purple, blue, or yellow colored hearts. Nor is there such things as hatred, unjust, bitterness, troubled, or wronged.

We were "pure."

My intentions for you were pure.

Your intentions for me were pure.

Originally, we all had a clear heart.

GaiGai!

It is not enough to love you for a thousand years. It is not enough to love you for a hundred thousand years. Love is love. Since the beginning our hearts have always been the purest white and will continue to be into eternity.

If there is no impermanence, no cause and effect, no Eighteen Fields, then what will there be? There will be a deep breath of fresh air.

Although I am a cultivator, I have my own character. I am still the crystal clear person from Moon River. The clouds may thin with the breeze, but I have not changed one iota.

GaiGai!

You said, "I know you are truthful!"
I answered, "I have always been frank."

Poem:

> *The brightness of the flower in full bloom*
> *And the brightness of the stars in the sky*
> *Emitting*
> *Light*
> *Will eventually dim*
>
> *The ocean swells*
> *The mountain sways*
> *Erupting mountains*
> *Angry oceans*
> *Caused many catastrophes*
>
> *But the hearts of Moon River beings are*
> *Forever free of waves*

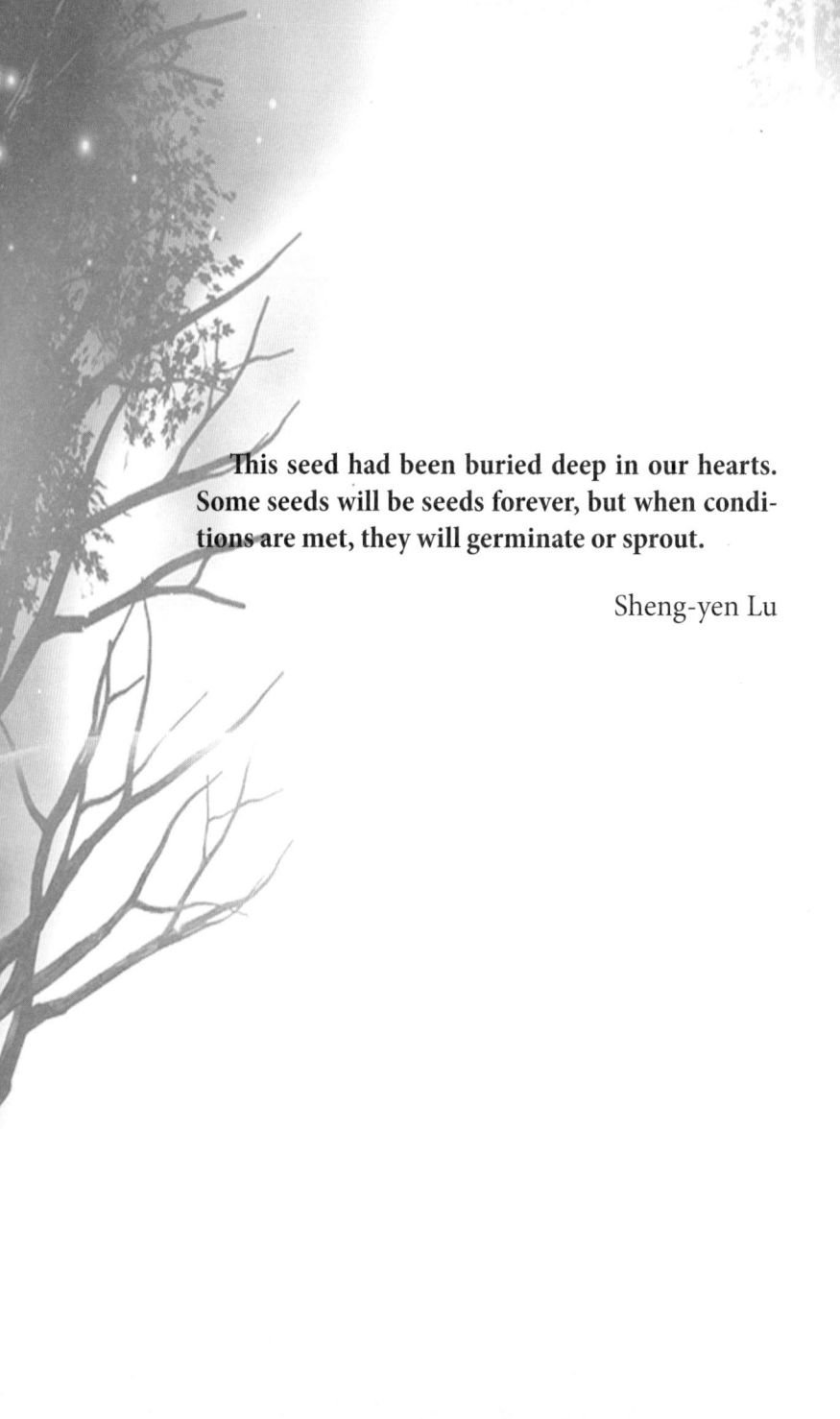

This seed had been buried deep in our hearts. Some seeds will be seeds forever, but when conditions are met, they will germinate or sprout.

Sheng-yen Lu

6. Standing in the Opposite Corner

When we were together at the Moon River, I had eighteen celestial ladies in waiting and you were the one in charge.

In the palace at Moon River were one hundred and eight celestial ladies in waiting, and we frequently made offerings to:

    Dakinis guarding the four directions.
    Dakinis of the eight directions.
    Celestial ladies of the twenty heavens.

The celestial ladies of heaven often sing "vajra songs," dance "vajra dances," adorn "vajra garlands, and play "vajra plays."

It is impossible to see the celestial beauties in the human world.

It is impossible to hear the celestial songs in the human world.

It is impossible to enjoy the celestial dances in the human world.

It is impossible to experience the celestial plays or games in the human world.

The *Agama Sutras* state clearly that celestial ladies and celestial palaces appear when a cultivator, who practices the Ten Virtuous Deeds, dies. This cultivator will be reborn into the heavenly realm.

He will go to heaven to enjoy his fortune without fright and pain or having to pass through the bardo realm.

GaiGai, at the Moon River, one of the scenic sites by the River of Heaven is your room, which is empty. And so is mine!

***

In this life, I have become the founder of the True Buddha School. I thought of looking for my GaiGai.
I searched among the crowds.
I searched among my disciples.
I searched within the six realms.
I couldn't imagine how else to search for you. I used my memory from previous lives, my feelings, our magnetism, but it was like fishing for a needle in the ocean or trying to find a needle in the haystack. Where could you be?
I remember the way you looked. You could not have changed too much for you were once a celestial being.
Truthfully, I have not been too anxious in finding you because of our affinity for each other. You will come to my side and I will come to your side. Then we will both be surprised because this whole time you were actually at the opposite corner.
Whichever corner you're in, you will unconsciously fill it with light.
I said, "This is the amazing ability of a celestial person!"
There is really nothing to be amazed about, for the light will follow wherever a celestial person is.
I said, "Don't always stand in the corner, for then your spirit can come forward and have more room to expand."
I really didn't need to look for you. For I was the king and you were the queen. This seed had been buried deep in our hearts. Some seeds will be seeds forever, but when conditions are met, some will germinate or sprout.
GaiGai!
You said, "I live this life for you!"

I am quite moved to hear this from you, but why have you been standing in the corner, not revealing yourself?

Poem:

> *You have been standing silently*
> *In the corner*
> *Then one day you said*
> *We have constantly passed each other by*
>
> *Then I became aware that*
> *I had not done anything yet*
> *Ah! You are an attractive celestial being*
> *I want to be whirled into you*

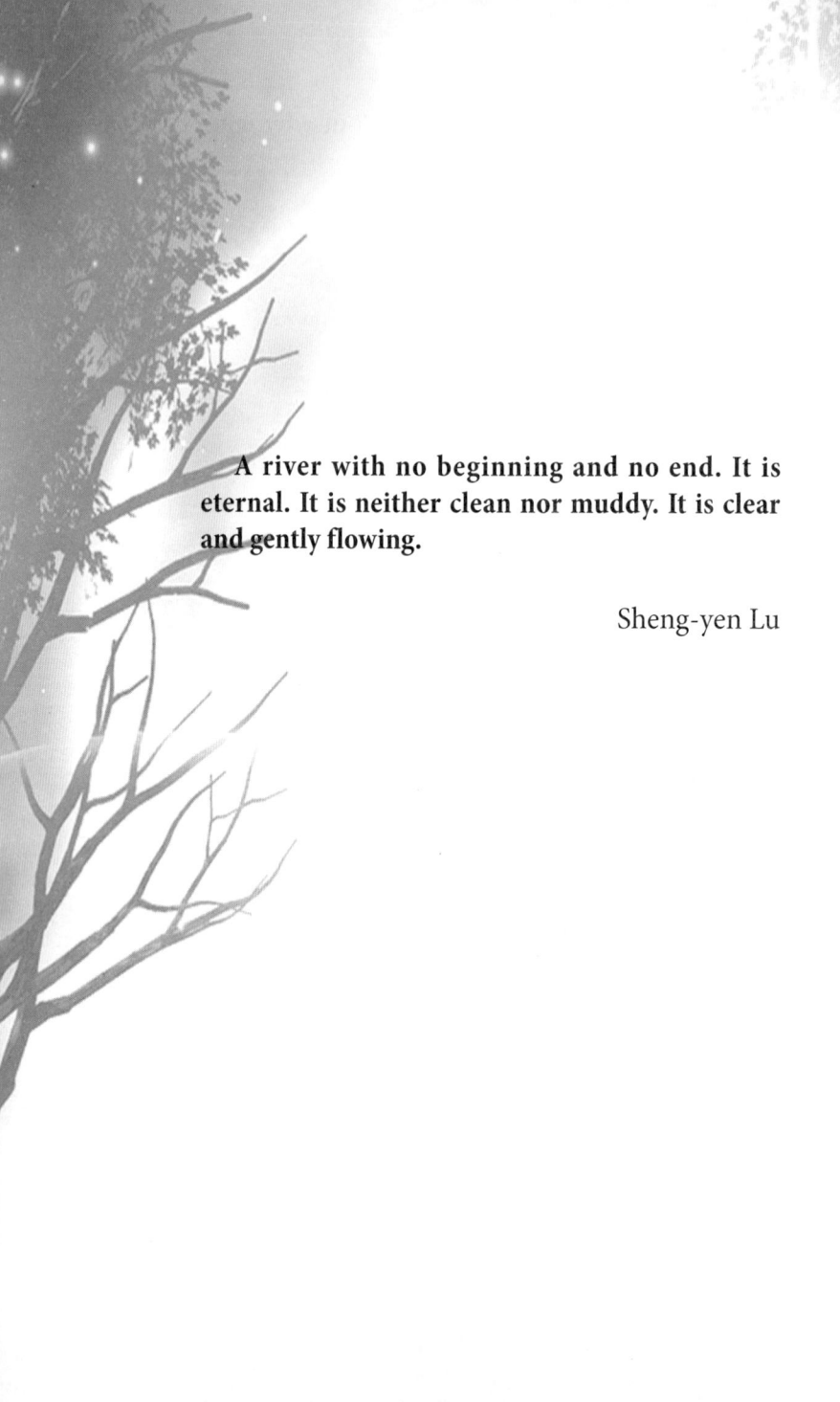

A river with no beginning and no end. It is eternal. It is neither clean nor muddy. It is clear and gently flowing.

Sheng-yen Lu

7. The Indelible Image of a Beautiful Lady

People who studied the concepts of Consciousness-Only understand that the senses of the eye, ear, nose, mouth, touch, thoughts, and ideas vanish during our deep sleep.
To know is to be "presumptuous."
Not knowing is "without memory."
And yet, we all have an eighth consciousness that is known as "Alaya." This root consciousness flows like a rapid current. This is the non-erasable seed of all our past memories.
As time passes, we humans will often forget. For example, how many of your classmates from elementary school, middle school, high school, and college can you remember?
Even memories of our best friends will, through time, be wiped out clean.
I am a cultivator. After I have personally realized my eighth consciousness, I can see you. You are that indelible, unforgettable image of a beautiful lady!
GaiGai!
Within the seed of my eighth consciousness is the remembrance of the Moon River. A river with no beginning and no end. It is

eternal. It is neither clean nor muddy. It is clear and gently flowing.

The remembrance of the Moon River is:

    Nonjudgmental acceptance.
    Eternal freedom.
    Pure and simple.
    Joyous and Spontaneous.

I am able to recognize you as the indelible unforgettable image of that beautiful lady because you are in the "Remembrance of the Moon River" and I am someone who has knowledge of previous lifetimes.

In my eighth consciousness (the tathagatagarbha), I sang a song, a song of happiness for both of us.

As I sang, swayed and dreamt, I visualized the image of the far away past coming forward with the celestial person that I deeply care for. Suddenly, the image of my love appeared.

The two images merged. One from the far away past and one is the present GaiGai.

This coming together exploded like thunder striking the earth. Clearing away to expose the original you.

I gazed at your eyebrows.

I gazed into your eyes.

I gazed at your nose.

I gazed at your mouth.

No matter how many reincarnations, gains, losses, partings, experiences, dreams, and etc. you will always be the lover's image from "the Remembrance of the Moon River."

GaiGai!

You will always be in the Remembrance of the Moon River, suffusing whiffs of mature but reserved fragrance.

Poem:

Who's able to have this perception
distinctly and clearly
Today
Shall we say with one word
Late

Remembrance of the Moon River
No matter how far away
Will always be in the depth of my heart
Obsess

Ascending to Enlightenment
My love for you
I can only say
Compensate

Relax a minute. You will find that your heart contains the mountains, rivers, and lights.

Sheng-yen Lu

8. The Lights Outside the Window

GaiGai! I told you before that every night before I go to bed I look out my window. I can see the lights from other high-rises and the coming and going of the headlights down below. The colorful lights weave into an illusionary world.

Then I say to myself, "This world is an illusionary world." Afterwards, I practice Dream Yoga and fall into a deep sleep and into the dream world.

I like to watch the lights outside the window because it is peaceful, colorful, and mystic.

Ha Ha! In this ambiance, it is easy for me to sleep peacefully. Yet, ever since you appeared, when I look out the window all I see is your face. I do not need to visualize your face, as your face naturally appears.

I know that the appearance of your face in the lights is actually a reflection of my heart.

I will say, "Good night! Sleep tight!" to the lights outside the window.

***

GaiGai!

You said, you seldom gaze out the window. Why won't you look out the window? There are mountains, rivers and lights outside the window and a blend of wonderful colors.

How long has it been since you've looked out the window? If you look out the window, your heart and mind will expand and feel happier and more carefree.

The depth and outlines of the rolling hills and mountains, the curves of the rivers, and the twinkling lights will take your breath away. Relax a minute. You will find that your heart contains the mountains, rivers, and lights.

I did not expect to find my aging face among the mountains, rivers, and lights.

Did you?

I hope your heart is not damp.

I hope your heart has not become moldy.

I hope your heart is not closed.

GaiGai!

Try opening the windows. Let the bright sun shine in. Let your spirit soar.

***

I am not like the other cultivators. Maybe people say that this is against tradition.

I am not willing to act the same as other monks.

I am not willing to be dispassionate because monks are to be dispassionate.

I am not willing to restrict my whereabouts because other monks do.

I am a monk who has the courage to write whatever I truly like.

Since you are the celestial being from Moon River, then I should have the courage to write what others cannot and will not write. I have always admired my own ingenuity.

Someone asked, "Are you writing about Shi Mu?"

I answered, "What do you think?"

Poem:

> *Passions are also cultivation*
> *Outside the window*
> *Has our spirits*
>
> *As long as there truly is*
> *Mutual attraction*
> *No need to hide*
> *No need to shut down*
> *It should continue*
> *Even in stormy situations*

If we grasp the present moment, then we have not come to this world in vain. Yes, for our lives would not be worthless.

Sheng-yen Lu

9. The Game of Seesaw

GaiGai! When I was at the Rainbow Villa, on the top of the mountain was a horizontal exercise bar, a parallel bar, a wooden shed, a space for broad jump, and a seesaw. I stared at the seesaw in a daze and found it inspirational.

A seesaw requires two people to play.
You are one and I am the other.
When you go up, I go down.
When I go up, you come down.
This creates the happiness of going up and down.

I wonder if, one day, you will be tired of playing and decide not to play anymore - if you would just get up and go. Then I would be sitting on the ground.

Let's say that I get tired first and decide not to play anymore. Then I get up and go. You would be sitting on the ground by yourself.

Oh dear!

The game could not go on. We would have to leave the seesaw because it could not be played by one person.

This leads me to think about the world in heaven.

Was this what happened at the Moon River? Were we tired of the game of seasaw and couldn't continue? Could it be the same in heaven?

How long can we play in the human world? Will there be one day, when you would say that you don't want to play anymore?

In this world, married couples are all in the game of seesaw. No wonder they can get tired of the game. As a result they get divorced, change players and remarry. One after one, over and over again.

At the Rainbow Villa, there is also a swing, which is played by one person.

It is also a game of going up and down.

No wonder there are also singles in this world.

Still a game of going up and down.

GaiGai!

These thoughts are depressing. But, this is also the reality in many current situations.

In reality, true love, loving the same person for a long time or forever is a very difficult deed.

Buddha said:

> Health will wane.
> Parting is inevitable after a gathering.
> Where there is birth, there is death.
> Obtaining nothing, obtaining nothing, obtaining nothing.
> Of course I have realized there is nothing to gain.
> I have realized there is no me.
> I have realized there is no birth.
> I have realized the true meaning of enlightenment.

I have learned to live in the moment.

GaiGai!

At this moment we are happy. We have lost ourselves in this moment of happiness as if we have reached the Pureland of Ultimate

Bliss.

If we grasp the present moment, then we have not come to this world in vain. Yes, for our lives would not be worthless.

We were together in heaven at the Moon River.

In this life, we are together.

We vowed to be together in future lives.

I don't care who got tired of playing on the seesaw. In our next life, and our future lives, we will continue. Alright?

Poem:

> *If we get tired of playing the seesaw*
> *We should give it a rest*
> *Skip a day*
> *Then we can continue*
>
> *We cannot be separated*
> *GaiGai!*
> *Don't hesitate*
> *Our vows are remarkable*
> *And wondrous*
> *Only because we understand this lesson*

After reaching Buddhahood, the absolute achievement, one has no restrictions or restraints, and can come and go as one pleases into the illusionary world.

Sheng-yen Lu

10. The Three Turnings of the Dharma Wheel

GaiGai! During my trip to Holland, I saw windmills. The windmills utilize the wind power for milling, turning grains into flour for food.

When I was in California, I saw the American windmill. These windmills have three blades, which were unlike the ones in Holland that had wider blades. Instead these windmills utilize the wind power to produce electricity.

GaiGai!

The windmills reminded me of the Buddha's three turns of the Dharma wheel:

First turn of the Dharma wheel - *Agama Sutras*.
Second turn of the Dharma wheel - *Prajna Sutras*.
Third turn of the Dharma wheel - the supreme meaning such as enlightenment (*paramārtha-gocara*).

For us cultivators, we can see the greatness of the Buddha's teachings through the wisdom and mundane practices for delivering all sentient beings by uncovering the ultimate meaning in Buddha's Dharma.

This is what we realized from the three turnings of the Dharma

wheel.
In looking at the windmills we see the wind.
In looking at the ocean we see the water.
In looking at houses we see the earth.
In boiling water we see the fire.

Most importantly, I see the love when I look into your eyes. Once you wore a pair of dark sunglasses and a hat that hid your face, but I could still see the love in your eyes.

I can see only goodness and beauty in your eyes. The beauty in your eyes is indescribable and the goodness in your eyes is unquantifiable. This kind of goodness and beauty continued from the Moon River and carried on to this life and to this moment. They truly, truly exist.

It is unfathomable to have two people with the same feelings at the exact same moment. How do you quantify it? How do you qualify it? I feel there are no words to describe it except that it is a continuous flow from the Moon River.

I wish to tell you that the three turnings of the Dharma wheel are like this. Buddha taught:

>Suffering
>Emptiness
>Impermanence
>Non-self
>(for Arhat deliverance)

Continue:

>Bodhicitta
>Six Paramitas
>Self Enlightenment
>Enlightenment of others

(for Bodhisattva deliverance)

Also:

Prajna
Consciousness-Only
Middle Way
The emptiness of the ultimate reality
(for obtaining the Buddhahood)

After reaching Buddhahood, the absolute achievement, one has no restrictions or restraints, and can come and go as one pleases into the illusionary world.

After I understood the emptiness of the ultimate reality, I achieved enlightenment and was able to see the true self and witness the Buddha-nature.

After reaching this state, I was not allowed to speak about it. Gai-Gai! In order to deliver you to Buddhahood, I became an ordinary person.

I am willing to be a sentient being.
I am willing to be an ordinary guy.
What is all this for?
All of this is for you!

Because there is no birth, one can tolerate everything. We are not afraid of being harmed. We are not afraid of any destructive slandering and will never be afraid of losing anything.

Sheng-yen Lu

11. Discovery of the Steely Glint

Most ordinary people are testy and rash. Very few are calm and composed.
In the human world, I have seen many people behave this way.
People lose control during an argument.
Obsessed in dominating a debate and become irrational.
Write polemically.
Even use foul language and become physical, causing bodily harm or death.
Unable to control one's temper for temporary short term satisfaction.
The heart is not at peace or content.
GaiGai!
In passing I noticed a steely glint in your eyes. I realized that you were angry before, you had arguments before, at one time your heart was not content.
Is this correct?
You said, "That was the past!"
I said, "We, cultivators, can only 'tolerate.' Tolerance to the utmost state is to tolerate with the dharma of emptiness."

The *Diamond Sutra* states: "There is no me, humans, others, or life." From "no ego" to "no birth."

Because there is no birth, one can tolerate everything. We are not afraid of being harmed. We are not afraid of any destructive slandering and will never be afraid of losing anything.

This "no birth" means, "since I have never been born to this world, there can be no me to be harmed, no me to be slandered, no me to acquire for and no me to lose from."

My face wears only a child-like smile.

GaiGai!

Your resplendent face is of heavenly grace, and your movements remind one of the flying deva of Dunhuang. Whoever sees you, will adore and admire you.

The sparkles in your eyes and eyebrows can be entrancing. But, I noticed a steely glint in your eyes that must be removed.

The winter has passed!

The hot summer will pass too!

The spring and autumn that we like will come soon. The flowers, grass and trees will bloom in spring. Even wildflowers and wild grasses will come alive.

The autumn's foliage can also bring many happy moments.

In autumn, maples turn red and yellow.

I have no idea about what happened to you in the past. I only know that at the Moon River I saw a scenic site by the River of Heaven. You were the heavenly being that was most close to me.

I said, "Remove the steeliness!"

You said, "Fine."

I asked, "Will you be angry with me?"

You answered, "No."

Merely this is enough. Quite enough.

Poem:

Looking forward to a peaceful life
Acquiring wisdom gradually
Forget the unjust of the human world
Your everlasting beautiful face
Is like an eternal bright light

You and I only have gratitude
Remove the anger
Throw it in the trash can
Or bury it deeply under the ground

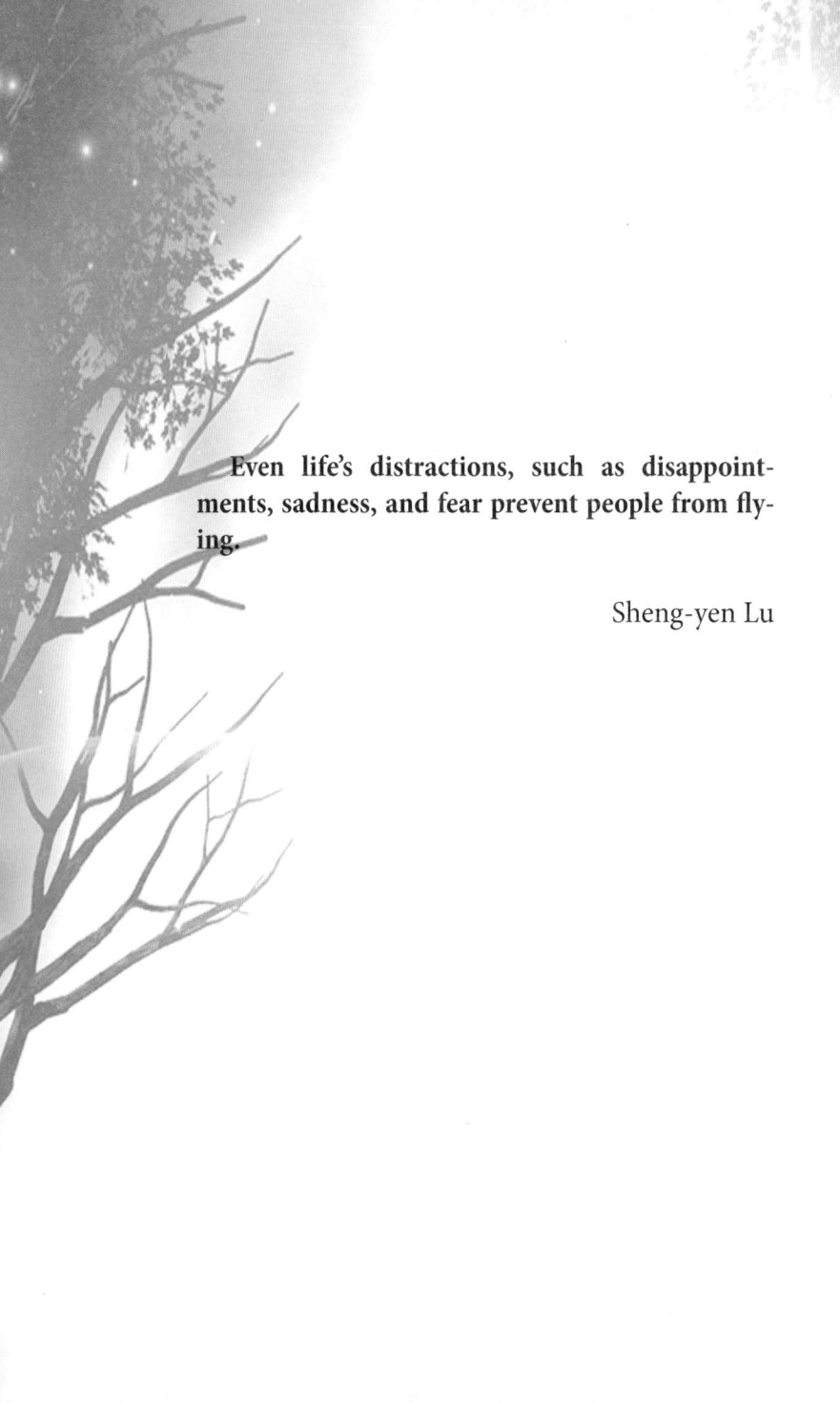

Even life's distractions, such as disappointments, sadness, and fear prevent people from flying.

Sheng-yen Lu

12. Flying in Space

We were able to fly at Moon River. We were heavenly beings, so our bodies were light.
GaiGai!
We were not birds, so we did not need to flap wings.
We were not dragonflies, so we did not need to extend our wings.
We were not bees, so we had no need to flutter the wings.
Only I know the secret of "astral travel," which allows the body to merge into space.
My intentions allow me to quickly go to different heavenly worlds without the need for wings.
The Christian God and angels all have wings. But their images are from pictures drawn from people's imaginations.
The reality is:
    Heavenly beings have no wings.
    We live on "air" and "ambrosia" (heavenly dews).
    We are made of air.
    Our ideas give us mobility.
    We use our thoughts to get us around in the Ten Dharma Realms.

In other words, we are similar to the wind, but faster than wind. We fly by our thoughts.

GaiGai!

We frequently flew to friendly worlds of all directions, along with our ladies in waiting. You could imagine how happy we were.

We glided freely in the vastness of space.

Every time we flew, our love for each other caused us to lean closer to each other. And with every time, our love soared in space.

***

We are different in the human world.

We eat food made of grains. Thus our bodies become heavy.

The components of the human body cannot merge with air. In addition we lack four natures:

> Our original nature.
> Our innate nature.
> Our pure nature.
> Our nirvana nature.

If we have these four natures, we would not just be heavenly beings but would also be buddhas.

Why can't people fly? The reason is not just because of our body parts, but also because of the following reasons:

> Worldly sensations.
> Knowledge hindrances.
> Apprehension hindrances.
> The obsession of me, people, others, and time.

Even life's distractions, such as disappointments, sadness, and fear prevent people from flying.

With all these hindrances how can people fly?

GaiGai!

Do you want to go back to the Moon River with me? At Moon

River we could lean against each other and fly around freely. How great would this be?

Poem:

Flying is wonderful and mysterious
What a way to admire
The infinite beauty of the great earth's landscape
GaiGai!
Why don't we hold hands
I miss the fun at the Moon River

We must be diligent in our practice
Do not be hindered by
Disappointments
Sorrows
Apprehensions
We must fly beyond and rise above it all

When we came to the third verse of "Amitofo," our minds started to oscillate. At this moment in time, our hearts reached the Pureland of Ulitmate Bliss.

Sheng-yen Lu

13. Let Us Happily Recite the Mantra

GaiGai! At the Moon River we happily sang in harmony. As I recall, the melody and lyrics of this song is of heaven. What kind of song?

A song that could cause the sensations of rising and falling. A song that enveloped the whole body-mind with love and peace.

The rhythm of the song oscillated from the highest point to the lowest point like a lotus flower supporting one's feet, swaying and floating along.

Like the pureness of the snow.
Like the light fragrance of the flower.
Like the calmness of the moon.
Like the weightlessness of the wind.

This does not fully describe it. It's like the falling of the red maple leaves in the human world - naturally and gently swirling along in rhythm.

As we sang at the Moon River all of our relatives of the Moon River heard us and they were just as happy as we were. They hummed along and were our choir of angels, joining us in harmony. They were also blissfully happy for this was the music of heaven!

I have seen *The Great Waltz* and *The Sound of Music*. They remind me of the spring wind combing through my hair and the warmth of the sun healing the wounded spirit, showering both the body and soul with happiness of a thousand years or a million years.

The name of that song is "Dreaming Dreams."

***

GaiGai!

We both once recited the same mantra simultaneously. The sound of Buddha was unique. It was pure, simple, and lifting.

I heard you had requested someone to put the music together and make it into a CD.

We randomly started to hum. When we came to the third verse of "Amitofo," our minds started to oscillate. At this moment in time, our hearts reached the Pureland of Ultimate Bliss.

We mindfully sang harmoniously.

Our minds merged to the beat.

Not quietly or rushed, chaotic moods gradually settled down.

GaiGai!

At the Moon River we sang together.

In this world, we happily recite the mantra together.

I did not know that you also knew the melody for the mantra recitation. You said that you produced that CD.

Also, you did not know that I could sing the mantra to that melody. It is really beautiful.

You said, "So, you have heard of it before!"

I said, "As long as it is yours, I have heard it all!"

I am touched. I think you feel the same.

Poem:

I am willing to sing with you
Singing together to reach the other shore
In our song
There is a moon

Singing un-provocatively
Singing dispassionately
No complaints and no pain
Just smoothly singing along
Unselfishly
Selflessly
This is our eternal wish

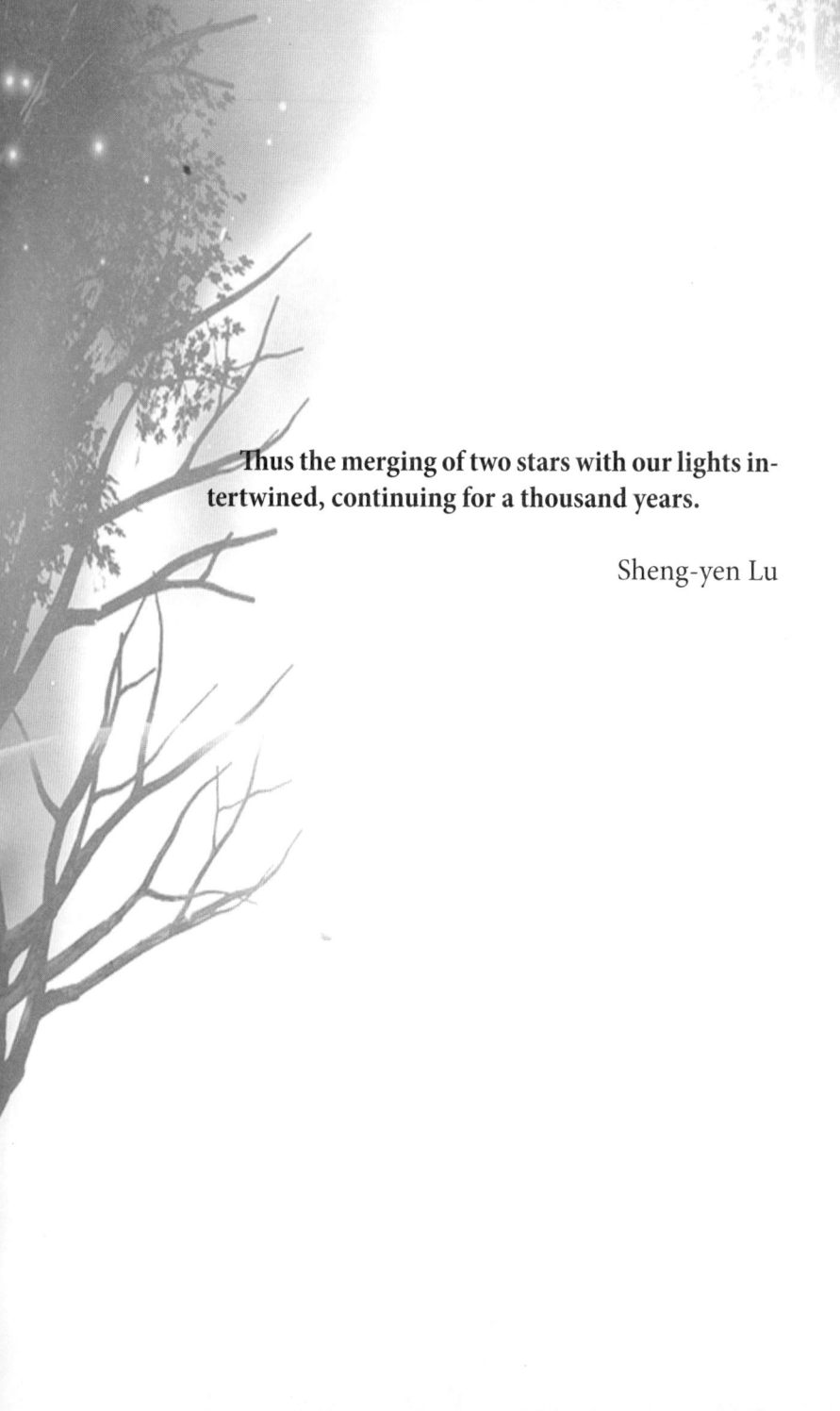

Thus the merging of two stars with our lights intertwined, continuing for a thousand years.

Sheng-yen Lu

14. The Stars on the Ground

GaiGai! In our past life at the Moon River we used to gaze at the stars in heaven. We looked at the stars and the stars looked back at us. Why? Because we were also stars.

All heavenly beings emit silver or white light. Sparkles of clear brilliance radiating splendor in the sky at Moon River.

GaiGai!

Do you know that at the Heaven of Light-Sound, heavenly beings communicate with light? They emit lights of various colors, some flashing, others straight and simple.

Amazingly, the colorful lights and different flashes are conversations between heavenly beings. This is wonderful!

This is substituting sound with light.

I was a star in heaven and you were a star in heaven. We were inseparable stars.

It is beautiful in heaven. Lights everywhere.

In heaven there is no work, no studying because whatever we need appears. Our prajna wisdom came from drinking the spring dew of the Moon River. Our wisdom would gush out like the spring water of Moon River.

When we see smoke, we know there is fire.
When we see grass, we know there are flowers.
When we see light, we know a conversation is taking place.
When I see you, I know there is gentle kindness.

At Moon River everything is well arranged and organized. There is nothing to worry about.

When I think of you, you would flow to me like the spring water. Thus the merging of two stars with our lights intertwined, continuing for a thousand years.

Gently.
Peacefully.
Happily.
Pure.
This is the blissfulness of the Moon River.

***

In this world, I once lived in Kaohsiung, Room 6513 of the Hotel Jindian. At night, I would open the window and look down toward the Hsitzu Bay.

Ah! The ground was covered with stars of different colors.

This was like looking down at the city lights of Hakodate from Mount Hakodate in Hokkaido, Japan.

GaiGai!

It would have been nice if you were there too.

Then we could lean against each other and enjoy the lights of the city together.

Watching the gathering and the separation of the little red and yellow lights of the cars.

Watching the fireworks ebb and wane.

We would just idly pass the time enjoying the beautiful night lights of Kaohsiung City.

You would say, "How beautiful!"
I would say, "Almost like the Moon River. The water at Moon River is full of sparkling stars!"
This is the most rewarding moment.

Poem:

> *Stars are the most beautiful poem of heaven*
> *Don't overlook them*
> *Study them in detail*
> *Every beautiful sparkling diamond*
>
> *You are that one*
> *I am this one*
> *Stranded together like pearls*
> *The Moon River threaded around you*
> *Making you the most brilliant light*

All the soft whispers and caring words
Are not as important as this
"I live for you"
These words are not a joking matter

Sheng-yen Lu

15. I Live for You

In this life, I feel that I am like the Mandala (altar) of the Vajrayana Buddhism. A Mandala of a strong and indestructible castle, square on the outside and round within, very beautifully colored, consists of four doors on each side, and non-penetrable security.

My relations (attendants) are dakas and dakinis. Above me are the lineage gurus, Vairocana Buddha, Buddha Locana, Amitabha Buddha, and Padmakumara.

Below me are my Personal Guardians, Five Vajra Vidyarajas, Eight Great Vidyarajas, and all divine troops that protect the dharma.

I would majestically sit in the middle of the Mandala, wearing the precious crown, and heavenly robe adorned in various precious jewels. I am Sheng-yen Lu the Living Buddha Lian-sheng and Grand Master of humans and heavenly beings.

This is how I visualize my heavenly body.
This is how I am manifested.
This is how I am established.
Until, one day, I met you.
GaiGai said, "I live for you!"
Wow! These words carried a lot of weight. Like an earthquake shat-

tering the walls of my Mandala, my beautiful castle disappeared along with my Personal Diety, my guardians, my attendants, etc....

In a flash, everything was gone.

GaiGai!

Now all is left is you and me.

I did not feel the pain of losing my Mandala. Nor, did I suffer from the loss of my castle.

Just because the power of those words.

Just because you were the Queen at Moon River.

Just because you and I are one.

Now you have entered my heart. You could enter without knocking. My mind is full of your image and you have conquered my "heavenly body."

It is ok that my castle fell.

We will rebuild a new one.

A castle for you and me.

In the center of this new castle, will be the heavenly body of you and me. This is the best Mandala.

I believe this is so.

You should also believe this is so.

***

GaiGai!

The words "I live for you" which you said to me are profound and carry a lot of weight. Heavy enough to break my lonely, but solemn castle.

This did not happen by chance, or randomly. This is a continuation of the lineage of the Moon River.

If I was a flower, I would not bloom for myself just because I was a flower.

You would be the bee.

For the flower would bloom for the bee and the bee would not leave the flower.

If I was a fish, I would not grow by myself.

Because I was the fish and you were the water, the fish could not leave the water and the water would not forsake the fish.

Poem:

>*All the soft whispers and caring words*
>*Are not as important as this*
>*"I live for you"*
>*These words are not a joking matter*
>
>*All the delicious food of various sorts*
>*No matter how scrumptious*
>*Will become tasteless*
>*Just because of this one sentence*
>*"I live for you"*
>*Makes my heart skip through eternity*

There will not be many hardships or set-backs, no despair, no awkwardness, no pretentious laughter, and no deception.

Sheng-yen Lu

16. The Sadhana of Kurukulle

When Guru Thubten Dargye was still alive, he told me that his Primary cultivation was the Sadhana of Kurukulle.

Because Kurukulle cultivation is the most effective in magnetism, the same power as Ragaraja, Kurukulle cultivation will attract many disciples.

Someone pointed out to Guru Thubten Dargye, "I haven't seen many disciple of yours."

Guru Thubten Dargye replied, "I attracted one disciple named Sheng-yen Lu which is the same as having five million disciples and their disciples."

This person was in awe!

Guru Thubten Dargye gave me:
    A picture of Kurukulle.
    Kurukulle's bow.
    Kurukulle's utpala flowered arrow.
    (Given to me in order to attract the masses.)

GaiGai!

Utpala flowers are flowers of respect. A lot of little pink flowers assembled together is its magnetism.

Utpala flowers are like the sunshine. Every little one has a brilliant smile on its face.

Shoot the arrow....

Whomever the utpala flowers touch, he or she will respect and love you, then harmony will appear:

    Presidents will be revered by the citizens!

    Artists will be hailed by audiences!

    Rich business people will be respected by their subordinates!

    Famous people will be idolized!

    Grand Master Lu would receive the welcoming of five million disciples.

***

GaiGai!

I never shot the utpala flower arrow at you. I have never and would never scheme to make you notice me.

You would never shoot an utpala flower arrow at me. I trust you haven't. You definitely haven't.

And yet, we have not passed each other by.

Only because our affinity for each other is a continuation from the Moon River which is natural, not from arrow shooting.

Our rendezvous is due to our past affinity not dependent on the cultivation of Kurukulle. It will not be affected by the process of birth and death, nor gathering and separation. It will not pass by unnoticed. There will not be many hardships or set-backs, no despair, no awkwardness, no pretentious laughter, and no deception.

We just came to meet at the same corner.

This is how the story started. It started due to the affinity continued from the Moon River.

It was not due to the cultivation of the Kurukulle Sadhana or from the arrows of utpala flowers.

***

GaiGai!
You are the flowers
I am the arrow
The flowers cling on the arrow
Completely inseparable

Poem:

> *It was not coerced*
> *Nor was it deliberately sought for*
> *Or consuming much time*
> *But*
> *It truthfully exists*
>
> *That is respectfully true love*
> *The heart is the boat aimlessly drifting on the river*
> *And yet*
> *You are the only one on this boat*

I will put you in my heart. With you filling my mind, you will forever hide in my heart! I will send you to the Maha Twin Lotus Ponds in the Pureland of Ultimate Bliss, or we could return to the Moon River together.

Sheng-yen Lu

17. Where Are You Hiding?

When we were young, we all played "Hide and Seek," a game where one person faces the wall, covers their eyes with their hands and counts out loud.

The rest of the players run to find a place to hide.

(1,2,3,4,5,6,7; 1,2,3,4,5,6,7; 2,5,6; 2,5,7; 2,8,2,9,3,10,1.) or count from 1 to 10.

Then begins the game of the cat seeking out the mice.

When we were young, we used to play this game often. We were very happy and always laughing.

GaiGai!

Did you play "Hide and Seek" when you were young? Were you the seeker who covered her eyes or the one hiding and waiting to be found?

I noticed that when I was young, I liked to pretend to be the cat, since the cat can be more relaxed. The person hiding was usually anxious about being found.

When I found them, I shouted "You're found."

"Ah! Finished!"

Now that I am a grown man, I don't know why my preference

changed. I am often tempted to go into hiding. In solitude where no one can find me.
Only because:
>Society is a big pot of dye (many colors).
>People scheme against each other.
>The strong prey on the weak.
>Friends are like tiger and wolf bandits.
>Disciples conspire against their guru.
>....

Heavens! This is a scary world. Even when one renounces and pursues cultivation, one continues to be harassed.

GaiGai!

You are the same. There is no safe haven for you. You wish to hide, yet where is a good hiding place? You have already suffered many injuries along this life's road.

You said, "I stayed hidden for eighteen years."

I said, "Really, how come I didn't notice?"

You said, "I stayed hidden well!"

I said, "No wonder, I couldn't find you."

I feel that since I found you in this life of "Hide and Seek," I should live in felicity with brightness surrounding me from now on.

Live well.

Cultivate well.

Encourage each other well.

I will put you in my heart. With you filling my mind, you will forever hide in my heart! I will send you to the Maha Twin Lotus Ponds in the Pureland of Ultimate Bliss, or we could return to the Moon River together.

Now that we found each other. Let us not part again!

Poem:

Hide, Hide, Hide, Hide, Hide
This is indeed a puzzling world
The matter in my heart
How can I tell anyone

Is it you who found me or
Did I find you
Doesn't matter, doesn't matter, doesn't matter
This delayed encounter
Still brought us various
Romantic rhythms
Extending and lasting forever

Then, we suddenly see old friends of many lives ago. We are overwhelmed with emotion and let the tears fall.

Sheng-yen Lu

18. The Tears in Your Eyes

I have shed tears more than once. Do you know why? My tears were not just for women. I did shed tears for Zhang Huangming, Master Jingxiang, and Master Liandian. I was overwhelmed with emotion because I met old acquaintances from past lives whom I was very close to. You see, our affinity goes back to the Moon River or from the Maha Twin Lotus Ponds.

We have been through many cycles of reincarnation. Meeting and parting, sometimes together and other times apart in story after story of both happiness and sadness.

Let's just say it is like "meeting old acquaintances from home!"

We have become worldly. We experienced many hard times. Like people swimming in whirlpools, we continuously struggle and exert our energy against the constant manipulation of our surroundings. Then, we suddenly see old friends of many lives ago. We are overwhelmed with emotion and let the tears fall.

GaiGai!

I know you also cried because I am an emotional person and you are an emotional person.

I am Sheng-yen Lu the Living Buddha Lian-sheng, I cannot be continuously shedding tears and be seen with red, blood shot eyes. I am a faithful Dharma propagator. I must be seen as energized and stable - confidently leading on as if nothing matters and taking responsibility for one's own actions.

This is how I present myself.

But within me, my emotions swell and sway so strongly they may crush a dam.

I don't want you to cry when you see me.

I don't want you to have red eyes.

I don't want you to sob.

I don't want you to shed tears that fall like the rain.

At this moment -

The roamers from the Moon River should meet with happiness, not with a depressed spirit.

You said, "Don't you know these are tears of happiness?"

I said, "I know."

But at this time, your crying creates a dilemma for me. Would you like me to sob openly to you?

Poem:

It is not that I don't place importance on your tears
I have also indulged in tearful sobs
Since nothing can be done, when tearful eyes meet with
Tearful eyes, isn't this a waste of time

Memories could bring about sadness
Causing our spirits to fly low

Put everything behind
Let's say hello to each other
Even soul mates and close friends
Are not continuously attached or constantly together

All the pores of the body will surreptitiously emit energy of sweet freshness. I am telling you, this energy can be food for the body.

Sheng-yen Lu

19. Never Thought About the Temperature

The temperature in Seattle, Washington is usually on the cool side. Therefore, most dwellings do not have air conditioning.
When it snows, looking out the window from the dining table, you see heavy snow flakes floating down like flowers drifting from space.
The drifting flowers are the snow.
The snow is the drifting flowers.
From time to time, when we wake up in the morning, the world is covered in silver just like the fairy tale land!
When the temperature drops to 20 degrees Celsius below zero, the snow turns to ice. Even the right pillar of the water fountain bends slightly from the weight of the ice. In winter months, the water in the fountain has to be drained. Otherwise, when the water turns to ice it could expand and crack the fountain walls.
GaiGai!
The winter days in Seattle is very cold.
I have lived in Seattle for twenty eight years.
There is also winter in Taiwan. However, summer is much longer. So in Taiwan there is at least one air conditioner in every home.
When the high pressure rises in the Pacific Ocean, Taiwan's tem-

perature will rise to 30 or 35 degrees Celsius. Sometimes even up to 40 degrees Celsius. Then in the eastern part of Taiwan, there will be dry winds.

Right after showering, a person begins to perspire again.

Some people shower five times a day.

One always feels sticky.

The news reports that one must drink plenty of water when outdoors to prevent heat stroke when the UV index is high.

GaiGai!

This is how hot Taiwan is.

Hot! Hot! Hot!

It's unbearable.

(The cold temperature in Seattle is unbearable, and the hot temperature in Taiwan is also unbearable.)

At this time, I remember the Moon River....

At the Moon River, no one thought about the temperature. It is very pleasant. Many people did not know that at Moon River the heavenly beings control their own temperature.

The temperature is whatever temperature one wishes it to be.

In heaven the temperature is whatever temperature one's body prefers.

It is natural that one's body feels the lightness and coolness of the environment. All the pores of the body will surreptitiously emit energy of sweet freshness. I am telling you, this energy can be food for the body. Heavenly beings consume energy as food.

GaiGai!

Can you remember the temperature of the Moon River? Can you remember the air of the Moon River?

Pure!

Refreshing!

Sweet!

Neither cold nor hot, celestial clothes do not need to be washed

because there is no dust.
GaiGai!
Shall we go back to the Moon River together?

Poem:

> *Should not be greedy for the worldly fame and*
> *Treasures*
> *And yet, religious societies still fight for it*
> *Then comes me, the coolest*
>
> *Hotness and coldness could hardly be normalized*
> *Unbearableness reflected on the face*
> *In this human world*
> *Temperature is either like a hot furnace or an icy lake*
> *GaiGai*
> *Why not return*
> *To the Moon River where love is natural*

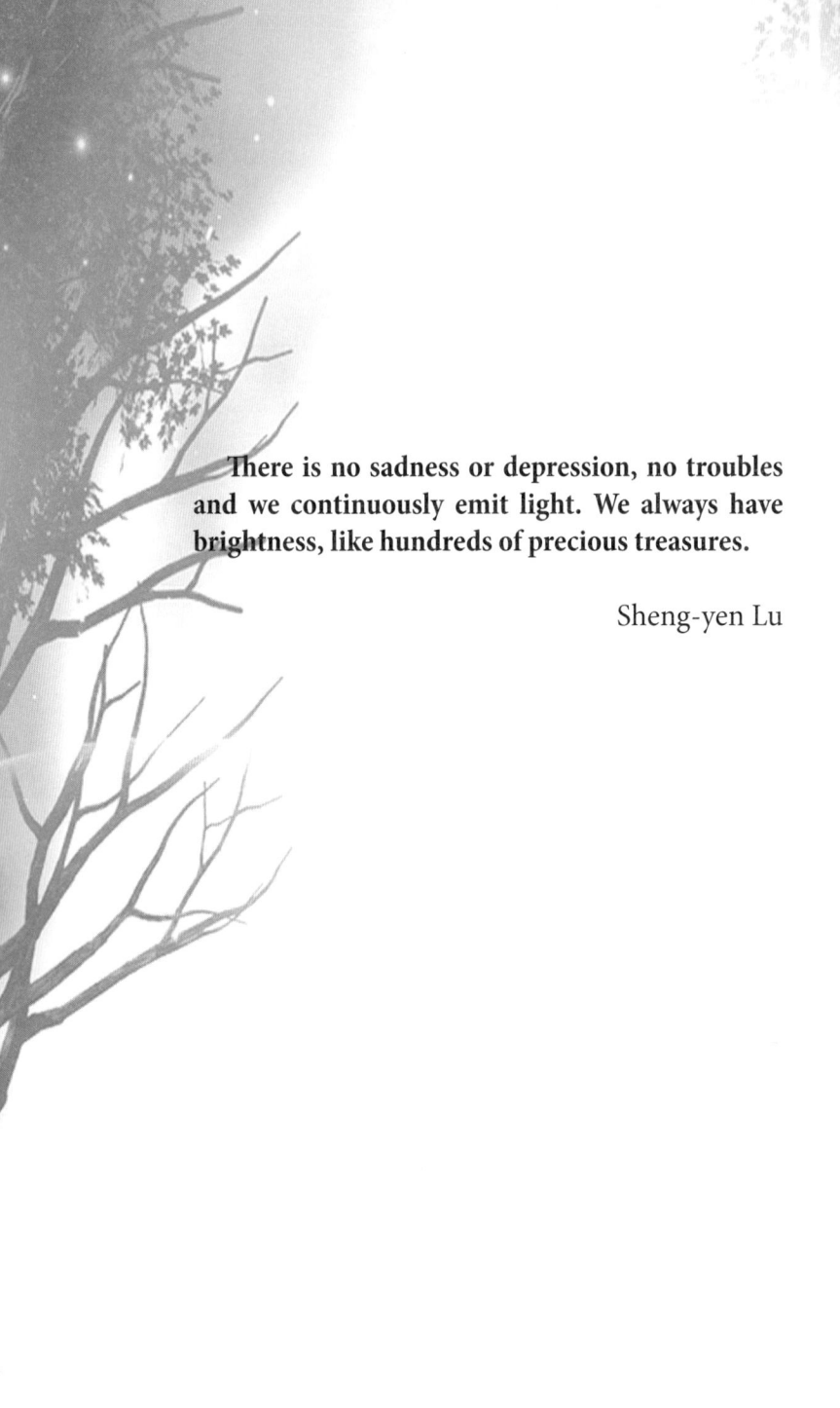

There is no sadness or depression, no troubles and we continuously emit light. We always have brightness, like hundreds of precious treasures.

Sheng-yen Lu

20. The Light at the Moon River

GaiGai! You asked, "Where does the light at the Moon River come from?"

I answered, "People don't realize that the light at the Moon River comes from the heavenly beings. The bodies of the heavenly beings emit light."

This answer truly surprises many people because most people think that light comes from only the Sun or the Moon. They do not know that heavenly beings can emit light too.

In the Buddhist scriptures, it often mentions light being emitted from the buddhas such as the immeasurable light from Amitabha Buddha, which is known by most people.

A buddha often emits light as far as ten feet. Why does the light emit ten feet? It is because buddhas emit such a strong and powerful light that most beings' eyes cannot withstand the brightness.

Buddhas, vajras, dharma protectors, dakinis, dakas, and all heavenly bodies can emit light.

Let me tell you, the "pearl net of Indra" is the source of light for the heaven of Indra and yet the pearl net is transformed from the heart of Lord Indra.

(This is not known by anyone in the human world.)
GaiGai!
Our Moon River (by the scenic site of the River of Heaven) is lit by the lights emitted from the heavenly beings residing there.

It is not from the sun.

It is not from the moon.

If it were from the sun, then inevitably there would be a big variance of temperature, either very hot or very cold. If it came from the moon, then inevitably there would be imperfection to the fullness.

The heavenly beings from the Moon River like to be happy. There is no sadness or depression, no troubles and we continuously emit light. We always have brightness, like hundreds of precious treasures. Honorable lights rise up to space and become the light of the Moon River.

The lights of our Moon River are:

> Laughter.
> Happiness.
> Fun.
> Joy.

The lights are comparable to the light of the Pureland of Ultimate Bliss. Wherever the virtuous being is, will be light as such.

I like:

> The lights from the Sumeru Light King Buddha.
> The lights from Dipamkara Buddha (Lamp Bearer Buddha).
> The lights from Buddha of Infinite Light.
> ....

GaiGai!

We only need to carry on being pure and clean, thus we will definitely be able to emit light.

The lights of our Moon River are from the Padmakumara of Shengyen Lu and yours. Our lights shine on each other and all around us to reflect the world of triumphant fragrant lights.

Poem:

The lights of the human world will dim
Because the sun will set below the horizon
The returning path will be dark and hard to recognize
This is night
Causing chaos by people's need to go to sleep

GaiGai!
The human world is different than the world in heaven
People have to rely on the sun for light
We don't rely on anything
Our lights are bright
Dharma lights are bright
The pure bright lights emit from the grand love of Bodhi

At this time, human sufferings, human hardships, human oddness, the coldness and warmth of the human world all dissipate.

Sheng-yen Lu

21. Singing Flowers

According to the Chinese calendar, I am 66 years old. This year my honorable disciples from all over the world will be celebrating my birthday approximately 20 different times, which is an especially fortunate event.

But, it has crossed my mind that for each year celebrated is one less year of this life. This way, our lives will be shorter and shorter as we continue to live.

One day, I will sing the "Graduation Song."

When the time comes, I will go back to Moon River, or go back to the Maha Twin Lotus Ponds, for I would have "graduated" from this life as a human.

GaiGai!

You are younger than me, so I will "graduate" first, and then you will "graduate."

You said, "I want to graduate with you!"

You said, "If you graduate, then I will graduate too."

GaiGai!

This is not possible. Everything is destined. Life's longevity varies with each individual. Therefore, graduating at the same time is not possible.

In the human world, when the Flame Tree flowers bloom, it is graduation time for students.

I have received many graduation diplomas and yet the last graduation diploma will be coming soon.

GaiGai!

Rest at ease, you will return to the Moon River and return to the Maha Twin Lotus Ponds. We will still meet.

***

GaiGai!

Do you remember the flowers and grass at the Moon River? One of the scenic sites by the River of Heaven? People would never know that flowers and grass of the Moon River are really flower fairies and rocking grass.

Flower fairies can speak and sing.

If I return, the flower fairies will say, "Master, you have returned" and then sing a "Worry Free Song." The rocking grass will line-up and bow deeply to respectfully welcome me back.

Flower fairies understand languages.

Rocking grass know respect.

Their color scheme varies, sometimes elegant and reserved, other times beautiful and calm. They understand your heart's rhythm, thus their songs let your heart spring with happiness.

At this time, human sufferings, human hardships, human oddness, the coldness and warmth of the human world all dissipate.

At the Moon River, a scenic site by the River of Heaven has flowers that understand languages and sing the rhythm of your heart.

At the Moon River, a scenic site by the River of Heaven has worry-free grass that can dance lightly.

Do you think you would like that?

Poem:

Flower fairies can sing
Your song of "do, ray, me, fa, so"
Thus, let your spirits fly
Happiness abounds
With laughter, ha, ha, ha

Rocking grass will bow
Ko, ko, ko, ko, ko
Swaying smoothly and lightly dancing
With the Song
This Moon River is worry-free.

You and I can
Enter this vast and limitless
City of Great Happiness

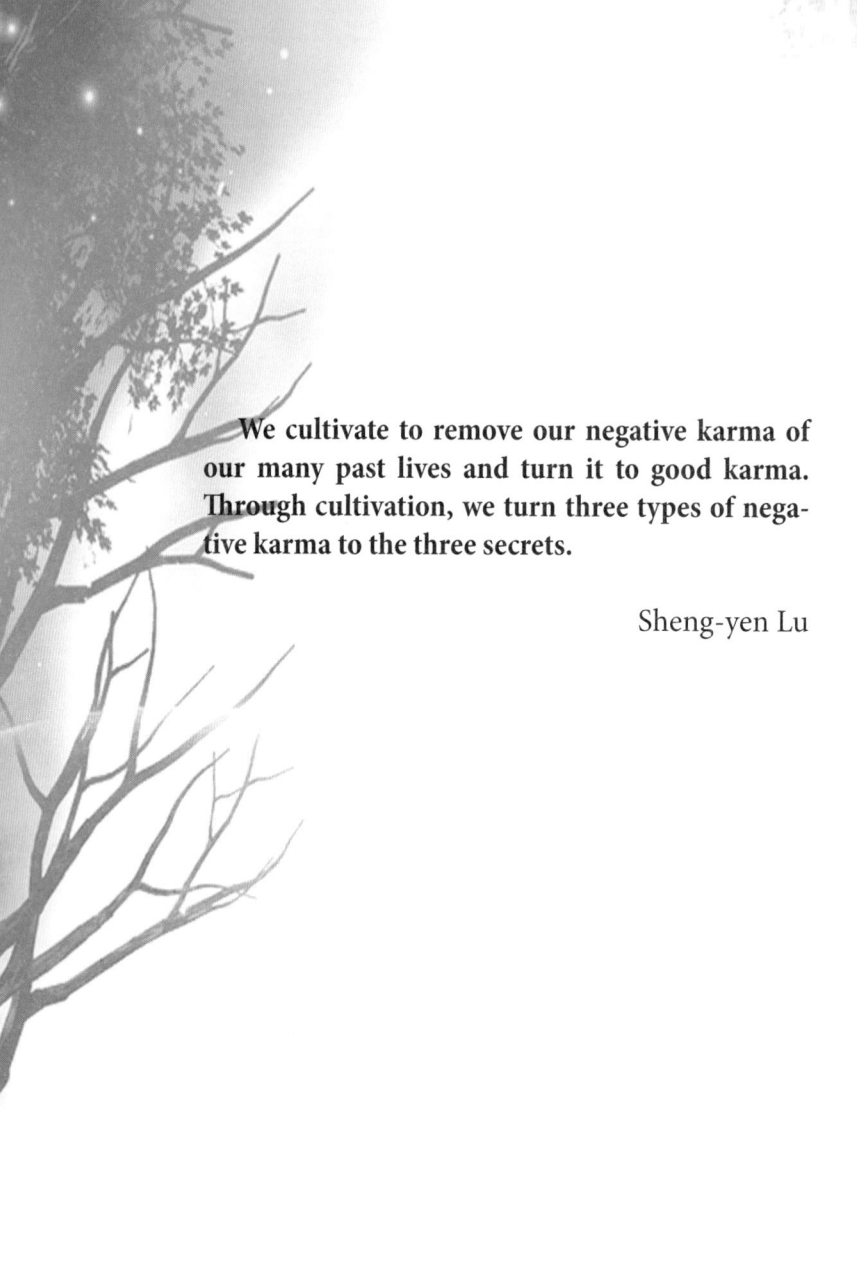

We cultivate to remove our negative karma of our many past lives and turn it to good karma. Through cultivation, we turn three types of negative karma to the three secrets.

Sheng-yen Lu

22. The Opening of the Dragon King Shrine

I once went to Hualian in Taiwan to consecrate the Dragon King Shrine at the Shibibu Temple. Its abbot is the son of Ji-o (Qiandai Shigu).
I recited:

    Consecration Mantra
    Liuding Liujia Divine Mantra
    Mantra of the Dragon King

When I arrived, dark clouds masked the sky. The Dragon King was in the sky moving the clouds and spreading the rain. A heavy rain then followed, splashing and hitting everything in its way with a bang.
Everyone said, "The Dragon King has arrived!"
The rain stopped during the consecration and the Dragon King entered the shrine.
Many people felt it. My consecration was very powerful. This "Dragon King" would guard the Shibibu Temple and protect the whole village from danger.
GaiGai!

At the Moon River, it never rains because the Moon River is a place in heaven where celestial beings stay.

Although it does not rain at the Moon River, "Mandarava flowers" do fall from space. When celestial beings are in deep meditation, when the heart is one with everything, the Mandarava flowers fall down from space.

This is called "Mandarava flower rain."

We know there are celestial beings deep in meditation when Mandarava flower rain appears.

Infused with the fragrance of flowers.

Infused with the freshness of flowers.

Infused with the pureness of flowers.

You will find that when one is in deep meditation, there will be fragrance from within as well as in the surroundings. This is the taste of Dharma.

GaiGai!

You asked me, "What are we cultivating for?"

I answered, "We cultivate to remove our negative karma of our many past lives and turn it to good karma. Through cultivation, we turn three types of negative karma to the three secrets. You are not the same person as before and I am not the same person as before."

Master Shen Xiu said, "Diligently rub clean!"

This is the purpose of continuous cultivation.

GaiGai!

Everytime I go to different temples of our many chapters of True Buddha Schools there are boys and girls who greet me with flowers, which always remind me of the "Rain of Mandarava flowers."

GaiGai!

Do you remember? We used to meditate frequently in the midst of the Mandarava flower rain and merge into one. Humans cannot envision such type of meditation.

Poem:

In the season of misty rain
Flowers rain in my heart
Remembering the time at Moon River
Our
Comings and goings
Our
Ups and downs

Sad sometimes
What went wrong
While roaming you
Must take care not to fall into
The three lower realms.

Rain continues
But you and I need not be depressed
Let the sunflowers bloom with radiance
We will fly together
Reciting the Mantra of Light

Thirty-two features of perfection and eighty types of fortuitous characteristics depict Buddha as the revered king who turns the Dharma Wheel.

Sheng-yen Lu

23. The Height of Heavenly Beings

GaiGai! You have always envied the handsomeness of a tall gentleman, conveying the likeness of a eucalyptus tree facing the wind. I agree that height is one factor in the handsomeness of a man.

However, you only see the outward straight tallness, but not the straight tallness within.

GaiGai!

You are not very tall. In fact, you are a little shorter than me. Therefore, you wish you were taller.

Really, what I regret the most is that I am not tall. I was at most 163 cm, and yet at 66 years old, I realized I have shrunk to 159 cm!

Aye! Aye!

I always mock my height, that I have to go through this life with a funny, ugly, fat, short body. I was always the last student in the lineup.

I have lived in America for 28 years and in America, because of my height, people may think that I come from the land of Lilliputians.

Even so, I do not envy other people's tallness, for I am a determined man. My spirits can dance and fly to great heights.

My meditation and wisdom are my wings, which can take me higher than anyone.

GaiGai!
You are the same. You are a little shorter than me, but I know your wisdom. The height of your wisdom is invisible. Many people, including me, can not measure up to you.
My height will not depress me.
Your height will not depress you.

***

GaiGai!
Do you know the height of the celestial being at the Moon River? Honestly, let me tell you, a "gilded body of eighteen feet."
Buddha has a "gilded body of eighteen feet."
Celestial beings also have gilded bodies of eighteen feet. We are all handsome, with thirty-two perfect features and eighty types of fortuitous characteristics.
Buddha said, "Thirty-two features of perfection and eighty types of fortuitous characteristics depict Buddha as the revered king who turns the Dharma Wheel."
We know:
Once, Mahamaudgalyayana flew to another buddha land. The buddhas there have immeasurable height. When they looked at Mahamaudgalyayana, it was like us looking at ants.
GaiGai!
Regrettably you and I have short bodies. But we are never depressed or deluded by it.
Our spirits sparkle light that can shine thousands of feet away.
At the Moon River, we stood eighteen feet tall!
You know? When my starlight body flies through the night, with refreshed power, my stature is big and tall.
We will always stand straight and tall.

Poem:

We walk faster and lighter than most
Our life has no beginning
And thus no end
Never decomposes

We may not have
Worldly fortunes such as
Youth, beauty, money, body and worldly status
But
Our wisdom is forever

Even though
The celestial bodies of the Moon River
Are roaming
We will never experience obstacles

The flying fish provide heavenly beings with such great happiness that people just cannot imagine.

Sheng-yen Lu

24. Flying Fish

In this world, it is common knowledge that:
   Fish swim in water.
   Birds fly in the sky.
   People walk on earth.
   Wild beasts crawl through forests.
GaiGai!
Did you know in Heaven, at the Moon River (scenic site by the River of Heaven), the fish swim around in space.
   Fish swimming in space?
   Fish of the animal realm, in heaven?
   What kind of fish are at the Moon River?
GaiGai!
The explanation is in *Amitabha Sutra*, describing the Western Paradise:

> In this land there are birds of all sorts of wondrous variegated colors: parrots, peacocks, kalavinkas and jivanjivas. All these birds bring forth harmonious songs day and night. Their songs communicate such Buddhist teachings as the Five Roots, the Five Powers,

the Seven Factors of Enlightenment, the Eightfold Path, as well as other teachings.

When sentient beings in this land hear the singing of the birds, they become mindful of the Buddhas, mindful of the Dharma, and mindful of the Sangha.

Do not think that these birds were born as birds due to karmic retribution for past misdeeds. Why not? In this buddha land, the Three Evil Planes of existence (as animals, hungry ghosts, and hell-beings) do not exist. In this buddha land, even the names of the Evil Planes of Existence do not exist, much less the realities. All these birds are the creations of Amitabha Buddha, fashioned in order to sing the sounds of the Dharma.

So there are fish in the Moon River, one of the scenic sites of the River of Heaven. In heaven, the river is created by light and the fish swim easily in light.

These fish are not from the animal realm, but created by the heavenly beings' minds because fish in water symbolizes unrestrained freedom and comfort. Fish are a fortuitous symbol for yearly extra abundance.

The fish of Moon River are the prettiest.
The fish of Moon River are colorful.
The fish of Moon River are free.
The fish of Moon River are picturesque.
The fish of Moon River are happy.
The heavenly beings of Moon River watch the fish and also become worry free. The welcoming sight merges with friendliness infused heavenly beings and fish. Heavenly beings feel the same as the fish enjoy the water.
The beauty of the fish is the beauty of heavenly beings.
The beauty of the heavenly beings is incredible and indescribable.
The flying fish provide heavenly beings with such great happiness

that people just cannot imagine.
We are never depressed, but always free and unrestrained.
We never wish to leave Moon River. Like the fish, we are able to fly around.
No need for wings, we can fly for we are in the vastness of heaven.

Poem:

> *Think of the human combative struggle*
> *Think of the human anger of unfairness*
> *Think of the human evil and treachery*
> *These thoughts make me weary, weary, weary*
> *These people cannot compare to the fish of Moon River*
> *How intoxicating are the fish of Moon River*
>
> *GaiGai*
> *All changes depend on understanding*
> *I like fish*
> *Flying like the moon in the sky*
> *Meditate a while*
> *Refresh with a pot of tea*
> *We are relaxed and free again*

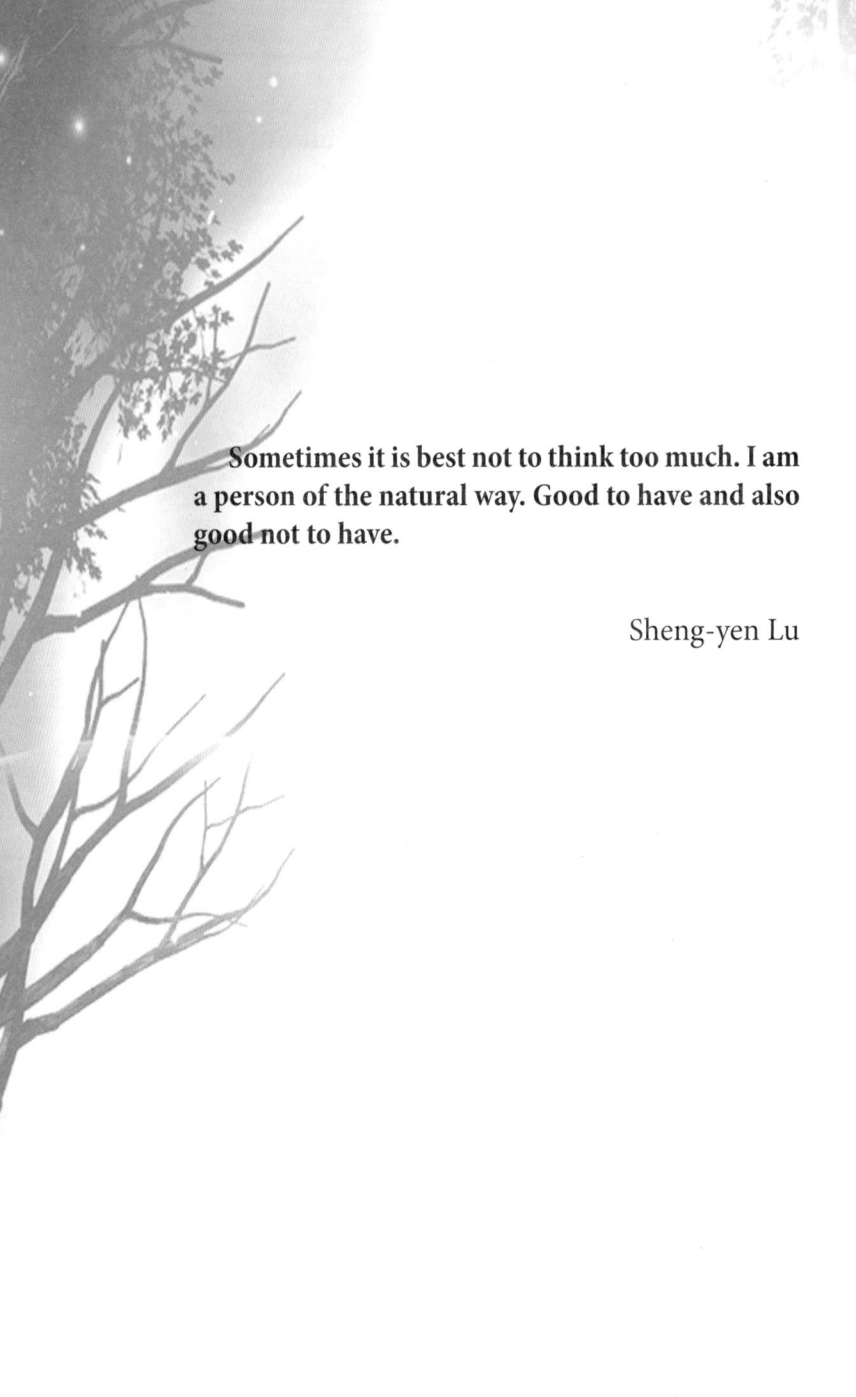

Sometimes it is best not to think too much. I am a person of the natural way. Good to have and also good not to have.

Sheng-yen Lu

25. You Are a Precious Rare Gem

I view people from Moon River as precious gems because he or she comes with talent. Especially you, who comes with so many talents. You are a rare precious gem.

I see that many people wish to be near you. Only because you radiate light, like diamonds, agates, crystals, corals, ambers, gold and silver. Many people suffer pain and despair for not being able to be with you.

It is natural for people to wish to be near beautiful women. So, because of this, beautiful women are the cause of many sufferings.

Some people die because of you.

Some people fall ill because of you.

Some people become mad because of you.

The one who has you also suffers because he has to pay attention to protect what is his. The worries of having and losing is another hardship.

Buddha said, "sufferings,"

Is truly like this.

I am also from the Moon River. This is why I know you are a rare precious gem.

However, I am not the same as others. People are all stubborn, but I am not stubborn.

I know "there is nothing to gain."

That is why concerning emotional affairs, I usually let them come and go naturally. I treasure it when it comes, but when it goes, I do not sigh. People never realize that the sweet feelings of affairs that never are realized linger most.

I also feel past feelings are truly very nice.

GaiGai!

I will always see you as a rare precious gem. From now until forever, you will always be precious.

Storing this feeling fulfills my heart.

***

GaiGai!
If you are a tree, I wish to be your leaf.
If you are the sun, I wish to be the moon.
If you are the sky, I wish to be a floating cloud.
If you are the ocean, I wish to be the fish.
If you are a boat, I wish to be the rower.

This is attachment. This is yearning. This is the co-operation of lights. This is a kind of consolation. This way, there will be a feeling of stability as well a force of independence.

Concerning cultivation…

Sometimes it is best not to think too much. I am a person of the natural way. Good to have and also good not to have.

Good whichever way!

GaiGai!

Can you understand me completely?

Poem:

Nature's way is
When the clouds become heavy, rain will follow
When the sun shows its face
The earth will have a renewed atmosphere.

Tearing when happy
Tearing when sad
Tears have only one indication
To radiate one's face.

The feelings of the human heart are
Forever swaying and fluttering
No need for words
No need for explanations
Because you and me are roaming

If there is despondence
If there is dust
Bury them quickly

I said, "Can you try to observe all occurrences as non-occurrences? Cultivators are frank and truthful with nothing to hide or fear!"

Sheng-yen Lu

26. It Happened to You

You said, "Something happened, that made me depressed and cold. The pain felt like all the bones in my body were breaking."

I said, "What happened?"

You said, "My heart is broken and it seems like the end of the world. My insuppressible agony has been transferred to complete coldness."

I said, "Don't be sad. We are Buddhist practitioners. We should not be sad."

GaiGai!

Life is like a big ocean and the waves are like the worldly affairs of our life. When the waves rush to the shore, they fall apart and then return back to the sea, and become part of the ocean again. This is the actual image of the ocean.

Thousands of waves.

Millions of waves.

They are the same when they return to the ocean.

Shakyamuni Buddha used to say, "All occurrences are not eternal," "All Dharma has no 'I'" and "Nirvana is peaceful." In the end, everything is transferred into the original truth.

Life's happenings and occurrences will come as waves upon waves, with no end. This is true for both you and me.

But when all returns to its "origin," it is as though nothing happened. Like the waves returning to the ocean, all the same.

 GaiGai!

Just like what happened before, in the end it all resolves into nothingness. Is it not so?

The ocean has many waves. After strong winds and big waves, it is still the ocean. You and I have to look at it this way.

I told you before, "Whatever happens, I will always be there to take on the burden. It will subside and become material for my writing."

You said, "I am not afraid. I will take on the burden. No one can hurt me, no one can mislead me. I have enough courage. I also understand the ocean and the waves."

I said, "The Buddha-nature is the ocean. The human world is the waves. You and I are in the waves of human world. In the end we will return to the ocean."

You said, "The Buddha-nature is the wind. The human world is the rumbling of the wind. You and I are roaming in the human world. In the end they are just images."

We both understand and clearly see through worldly affairs, people, things, etc.

Let us remember the special scenery of the Moon River and its eternal radiance and beauty.

I said, "Can you try to observe all occurrences as non-occurrences? Cultivators are frank and truthful with nothing to hide or fear!"

Poem:

Waves upon waves of worldly affairs of suffering
Intensifies us for cultivation
The taste of bitterness
Propels us

Waves and oceans
Are of the same in origin
Let us enjoy
Their differences
You need an exit for the spirit
To find the pure land
At last you will understand
Holding hands strolling on the beach

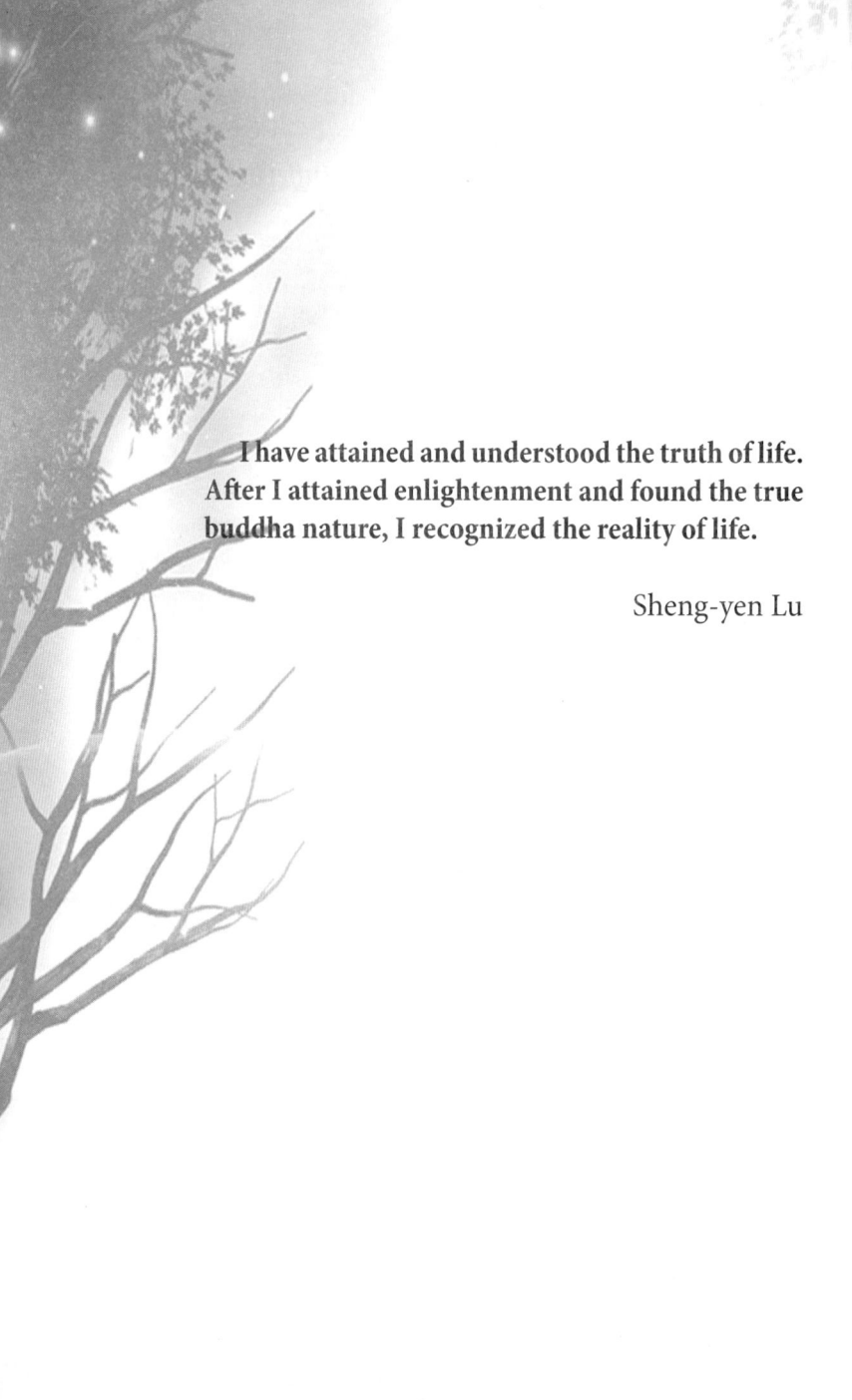

I have attained and understood the truth of life. After I attained enlightenment and found the true buddha nature, I recognized the reality of life.

Sheng-yen Lu

27. Liking Everyone

GaiGai! You said, "This is a good person. That is a bad person!"
I said, "I like everyone."
You said, "You don't differentiate between good or bad?"
I said, "I don't differentiate."
You asked, "Aren't there certain people that you like?"
I said, "GaiGai! I will tell you about this at a later time. We must wait for the right moment!"
What I mean by this is: Bodhisattvas like everyone and do not mind if others don't like them back.
You said, "This is on such a higher plane!"
I said, "Ordinary people are not able to like people who slandered them, or cold people who despise them, or people who have animosity towards them, or people who are overly defensive or selfish, or people who hate and discriminate, or bad people, or people who are self obsessed. Would you be able to?"
You said, "I couldn't!"
I said, "Bodhisattvas have to deliver sentient beings. In spite of people's imperfections, we still have to respect their strong points. If we like everyone then others will like us too."

If you do not like everyone, how can you wish that everyone likes you?

With GaiGai and I!

Our attraction is extra-ordinary!

It is like a satellite orbiting a planet.

It is like the planet's force keeping the satellite in orbit.

GaiGai!

In this lifetime, it seems like I am the injured party, but actually, it is not the case.

Why?

I am using "Non-self" and "No birth" to bear this all.

If there is no self, then where is the harm?

Why are there ideas of "Non-self," "No Birth"? My answer is "Buddhadharma"!

I have attained and understood the truth of life. After I attained enlightenment and found the true buddha nature, I recognized the reality of life.

This world appears to be unfair.

In the Buddhadharma all is fair.

In fact, there is no fairness and unfairness. This is why I like everyone.

Put this way, do you understand?

Poem:

Was there ever harm to oneself
Bodhisattvas' love for sentient beings knows no hesitation
Whose rudeness
Whose unkindness
Buddha-nature is ubiquitously omnipresent

Between you, me, and them, who is the worse
Bodhisattva said
Wish to deliver all sentient beings
Can't differentiate good
Can't differentiate bad
This is equanimity of heaven and earth

The affinity between you and me
Is excellent kindness! excellent kindness!

You know that in this life, I have been misunderstood numerous times. Negative publicity never stops. It is fortunate that I am mentality resilient or else I would not have been able to survive.

Sheng-yen Lu

28. The Feeling of Being Misunderstood

In this world, misunderstandings can never be justified. Many people suffer disappointment from being misunderstood. They wish to explain, but to no avail, for no one believes or cares. Often times they can not overcome this ordeal and look for a way out.

Shakyamuni Buddha was a revered living buddha. His every word and action was epitomized by people and heavenly beings and yet, towards the end of his life Devadatta also misunderstood Shakyamuni Buddha. He not only left the Sangha himself, but also split up a fraction of monks and disciples. This is caused by the misunderstandings of Devadatta.

And there is....

Devadatta's arrogance.

Devadatta's ambition to lead the Sangha.

Devadatta's cultivation of clairvoyance.

Devadatta's antagonism towards Buddha Shakyamuni.

Devadatta thought Shakyamuni Buddha should not receive offerings, wear nice clothing, reside in nice house and eat good food.

So, Devadatta rebelled.

Shakyamuni Buddha wished to explain, but Devadatta would not listen. So the Sangha split.

I believe Shakyamuni Buddha was saddened by this, but what could he do?

***

GaiGai!

You know that in this life, I have been misunderstood numerous times. Negative publicity never stops. It is fortunate that I am mentality resilient or else I would not have been able to survive.

I have never given up my faith.

I have never given up on True Buddha School.

I have never given up on the masses.

I have never given up on saving the world or anything else for that matter....

Even in the midst of deep misunderstandings that could not be rectified with explanations or may have even considered to be true, I still insist on continuing, going through life with these misunderstandings.

So, not caring about being misunderstood, I still live my life without necessitating suffering.

Because I have achieved enlightenment and attained realization, I perceive it as merely an "imaginary life" and "imaginary feelings."

GaiGai!

In this world, is there anyone that has not been misunderstood? Misunderstandings are unavoidable and happen so frequently, that they render explanation unnecessary. Just continue to be true to yourself and not worry about being misunderstood or not.

You are not afraid of being misunderstood.

Of course, I am not afraid of being misunderstood.

Would you say this is correct?

Poem:

The Buddha said
This world is a world of unbearable sufferings
Tolerance, tolerance, tolerance, tolerance, tolerance
Insult, insult, insult, insult, insult
There is no limit

I advocate to give up completely
To not care
Who cares about misunderstandings
I am still me

No need to suffer
There is no other, no me, no life, and no people
Not caring about not caring
Mindless of mindless
People ask for my opinion
My only answer is "Yeah"

Therefore, when a Dharma King is present, all spirits offer support. Thus, many strange and uncommon happenings appear on my behalf.

Sheng-yen Lu

29. Charming of the Five Blessings

GaiGai! While I was in Hong Kong and Macau for my Dharma Talk Tour in July 2010, Master Lianxin and some other masters in Hong Kong invited me to a restaurant for dinner.

What I wish to tell you is that something very strange happened.

It happened on the night of the 27th after we finished eating and just after I left. Out of nowhere, five bats flew in. Symbolically, bats in China are a symbol, especially if there are five, which represent the five blessings.

(In the center of Wan Chai District in Hong Kong where could five bats come from?)

What was even stranger was that the five bats flew around the seat that I had sat in for quite some time, as though they did not wish to leave.

The owner of the restaurant was astonished at this sight.

1. Where did the bats come from in a busy city?
2. Why were there exactly five?
3. Why did they fly only around the seat that I had sat in?

The owner thought this was an auspicious sign "the charms of the five blessings!"

As predicted, from then on the restaurant was packed all the time and business prospered. They thought I brought them this good fortune.

The red banner of "Welcome Living Buddha Lian-sheng to Hong Kong" was left hanging because they did not want to remove it.

GaiGai!

What caused this to happen? It is because I am a cultivator. I have attained "Great Bliss," "Radiant Light," and "Emptiness." I have achieved enlightenment and attained realization. My achievements have surpassed the level of the heavenly realm.

Therefore, when a Dharma King is present, all spirits offer support. Thus, many strange and uncommon happenings appear on my behalf.

Another example:

During the Dharma Talk at Rushi Chapter in Macau, it was thundering and pouring rain outside.

Then the rain stopped.

But the thundering continued.

Everyone thought it was a sign of auspiciousness.

The titles of the temples of True Buddha School all contain the words "Thundering Temple" within the title. Thunder predicts that a True Buddha Thundering Temple will soon be erected. This is the welcoming from the God of Thunder of the Ninth Heaven.

GaiGai!

For me, as long as cultivation leads to fruition all blessings and auspicious events will follow, because spirits will follow. It definately is an "auspicious day, auspicious night, and eternal auspiciousness" for I am an auspicious person.

This is:

Letting all things be, let nature take its course.

Spiritual happiness springs forward.

Earth's mountains and rivers sing along.
All spirits offer a victory dance.
Ha! One only needs to "diligently cultivate" to reach "abundant fruition."
GaiGai!
Cultivation is the most important.

Poem:

>Don't have to change one's lifestyle for cultivation
>Just let the buddha sit in the center of your heart
>Don't forget to chant
>Spiritual response will happen naturally
>
>Chant while strolling
>Chant while reading
>Chant while listening to music
>Chant while dressing, preparing food, living, traveling
>Cultivation is like this
>It is never boring
>
>GaiGai
>All things natural are nature
>Buddha's and bodhisattva's pure light will validate

The environmental influences can only restrict the body, but never the mind.

Sheng-yen Lu

30. Smiling Voices

Remember our time together at the Moon River? We only needed to look at each other, to feel the closeness of our hearts. Celestial beings only need to gently hold hands to merge into one. Our caresses are the smiling voices.

I can feel your closeness. No matter how far away, or how long ago, like I said before, it feels just like the present. It is like a dream and yet so real.

We just love to laugh like this.

Laughter is a release. Laughter can relieve burdens. The smiling voices of the celestial beings bring the utmost happiness.

So, you look out the window at the sky, trying to remember "stories of the Moon River" and search your memories.

You asked, "Is the Moon River within the earth, mountains, and rivers?"

I answered, "The nights of mountains, rivers and lands contain the constellations on earth."

You asked, "Is the Moon River far away?"

I answered, "It is right in front of us."

We both smiled. Yes, at this moment, it is just like Moon River. The remembrance of the Moon River always includes our longings and our disappointments. Longing to once again return to the wonderful moments.

And yet, we met at a foreign country!

All is an illusion.

All is so real.

We began our smiling conversations again.

I wanted to tell you that no matter what happened before, and no matter what we possessed, they are of no importance. The important thing is, at this moment, we are having a smiling conversation which brings about happiness!

You said, "I feel like I have arrived at the Western Pureland of Ultimate Bliss, the Maha Twin Lotus Pond."

I said, "Same here."

What I wanted to tell you is....

The fears, suspicions, disharmonies, and dejections of this world do not have a place.

Don't hesitate.

The environmental influences can only restrict the body, but never the mind.

Don't worry about tomorrow.

If we continue this way, you will discover a world that truly belongs to you.

We still have a lot to say, but conversation is not necessary. For all we need is to look into each other's eyes. Our hearts will be joyful and smiles will appear on our faces.

Poem:

For smiles to appear on our faces
No need for conversation
Similar to the deaf and dumb
There will be sweetness in our eyes

Obsessively swallowing the continuous rain drops
That night
We both swallowed a mouthful of water
Our pupils melted into delicate smoke

There will be a day
Forgetting the outside surroundings
Forgetting the eyes of the people around us
And entering the smiling conversations of forgetting oneself
At this time and moment
All words are excessive
"Moon River" and "Human World" are connected

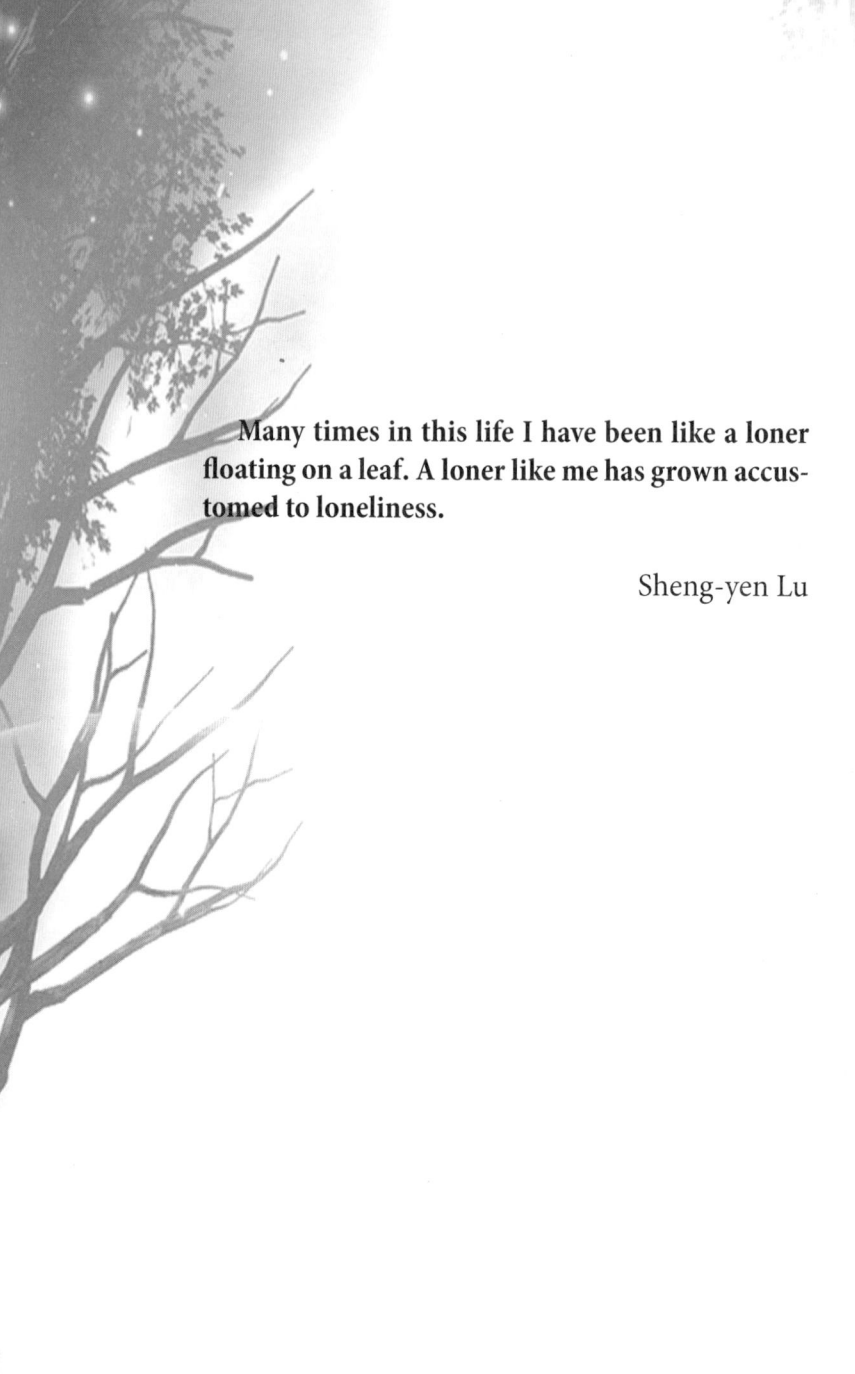

Many times in this life I have been like a loner floating on a leaf. A loner like me has grown accustomed to loneliness.

Sheng-yen Lu

31. Good Times Never Last

There is a song with the verse, "Flowers don't bloom forever and good times never last."
The Buddha also said:
"If there is aggregation then there is separation."
GaiGai!
This is what worries us, but we also know this day will come soon. We often think about this problem. The result is always the same. The answer to this problem is always blank.

Do you see the Flame Tree flowers? Its small petals flying in the wind, like small hands waving goodbye!

You return to your origin.

I return to my origin.

This is life. There will be a time when we won't be able to see each other. This is the separation from love ones, which is one of the eight sufferings.

In my books, I have never written about "love" because it is not necessary to elaborate on love, or talk about love, or specifically write about it in a book. It is not necessary.

One smile is enough.

One handshake is enough.
One glimpse of acknowledgment is enough.

It is present in the atmosphere for it comes from the depth of the heart, turning into a web of magnets. The rhythmic beat of the heart brought a tinge of bitter sweetness, like yeast that expands exponentially, just like this.

We do not shed tears!
We do not cry!

Because we know this human life is not forever, impermanence is natural, many incidents are like this, and nothing in this world is forever.

Many times in this life I have been like a loner floating on a leaf. A loner like me has grown accustomed to loneliness. I will treasure this warmest act with you which brought me satisfaction to this lifetime performance of mine.

What else could I ask for?

"Very happy, very fortuitous, very satisfying." This is what we both wish for. And then what? We don't dare think further.

At this time, we should settle down and cultivate and then dedicate this merit.

Let water flow with ease.

I, this enlightened monk, know very well "there is nothing to have," know very well "there is nothing to gain," know very well "there is nothing to own," know very well "advance, or retreat," so let's dedicate this merit to the Moon River.

Let's meet again at the Moon River!
Let's meet again in Heaven!

Maybe we will meet in another world. It is not a case of maybe, but we will meet for we have the same magnetism and we can enter the home that is ours forever.

Poem:

I don't remember why I wrote this article
I totally forgot myself
Rumbling in this earthly dust
How does one explain the emotions of an image

You can also play the rhythm of magical tune
Your ten long fingers
Playing on and on
Every musical note
Melting into my spirit

When will life awaken
Where will our rowing paddles take us
Let us cultivate well and dedicate the goal
To emerge together from this weariness of worldly affairs

I treat all sentient beings equally, without discrimination, and am approachable and never cold.

Sheng-yen Lu

32. Charming Smile

GaiGai! Let me tell you. Your charming smile, which attracts many people, is the reason why you are so popular. Your happiness radiates enchantment.

Frankly speaking, I like smiling people. I always feel more intimate when I am greeted with a smiling face, which closes the gap between being strangers to being acquaintances.

I feel I need to improve. I am a straight forward person. I also quite often laugh out loud. But True Buddha disciples make mistakes. The misdeeds freeze my face.

Frozen is not good, for eventually it will become frozen popsicles. Unable to defrost is my regret.

Time and again....

When I see a frozen face, I feel sad.

When I see a frozen face, I feel bored.

When I see a frozen face, my feelings freeze too.

I don't like frozen faces, and of course, I would not like to have a frozen face either.

So, I want to be like you and have a charming smile on my face that comes from my heart.

I know I should not have a frozen face. Maybe, it was brought on by too many trivial and mundane affairs. My face became unemotional, hard, and inflexible.

GaiGai!

I know this is wrong. I must correct this.

I love everyone.

I treat all sentient beings equally, without discrimination, and am approachable and never cold.

I like to see your charming smile. Your charming smile melts away the snow and brings spring back again. Everything livens up and happiness returns. Unexplainable affections naturally arise.

I treasure the time we spend together.

I treasure your affection.

I will always keep your charming smile in my heart throughout this lifetime. No, No, I mean in all my lifetimes forever.

I like the Moon River, for heavenly beings have only happiness.

There are no frozen faces at the Moon River.

At the Moon River, there are no altercations, only happiness.

GaiGai!

Your greetings, "Grand Master! Wish you well!"

Your charming smile and humble greeting is the pillar of my day's work.

I say, "Thank you!"

Poem:

All the distractions of the human world
Brought out anger, sorrow, and happiness
And yet, as cultivators
We have to put down anger and sorrow

Praise your face
Like your charms
Your smile
Is the spring breeze

Let me pick up the drawing pencil
To capture this moment
Yet I know drawings would not do justice
For a charming face encompasses much more
I would never be able to put it all in a picture

Bodhisattva's feelings don't differentiate old age, middle age and young age.

Sheng-yen Lu

33. Purely Fictional

Some people think, this book, the *Remembrance of the Moon River* is a work of fiction created from the mind of Grand Master Lu. In today's society people may believe that Grand Master Lu is only sleep talking.

Some people believe as follows:

Moon River ------- is a heavenly world where no one has been.

GaiGai ------- is an imaginary person.

Writing ------- is fictional - just finding a person to talk to about one's ideals and hopes.

Grand Master Lu ------- is an old man of 66 years who wishes to use exquisite writings of emotional feelings as a challenge to his youthful past. The result is this book.

In my opinion, I respect this reader's observations. It is true that I have not written articles of emotions for a long time. I am not a young man with a heart full of anticipation for spring. I am at a respectable age.

And yet, looking back, there are many memorable moments, people, and feelings from my past where the details are so vivid.

Therefore, the past clings tightly to you. And writings can also cling

tightly to the past.
   Moon River ------- is from memories of many lifetimes.
   GaiGai ------- is from memories of many lifetimes.
   Writing ------- is a way to record these memories.
   It can be fictional and it can also be real. I like to keep a record of the past, the present, and the future together to become the garden of fragrant flowers of life.
   I am getting old.
   I am copiously emotional.
   As if, near the end of my life, I can still return to the youthful beginning.
   In this society there are a lot of stressors and irritants. If recorded as it actually is, it would be a mundane record without harmony or rhythmic music.
   Maybe emotional expressions release oneself as if being youthful again.
   Don't think about whether it is fictional.
   Don't think about whether the characters are real or make believe.
   Don't think about whether the stories are real or not.
   In the days to come, I could still at any moment, may be in my 90s, write a lot more emotional love letters!
   My life and emotions can never be categorized or restricted. Youth will have feelings of youth. Old will have feelings of old. Bodhisattva's feelings don't differentiate old age, middle age and young age.

Poem:

Often forgetting my age
Holy disciples, please don't remind me
That old age
Should negate the emotional feelings of the youth

Who's to tell my heart is still fluttering
Even with clarity of the dharma
The invading shadows from afar
Is at peace in meditation along with each verse of the mantra

GaiGai
Still cannot miss your lovely image
Is it fictional
Is it real
Half is a green mountain and half is a white cloud.

Every peak of the mountains
Every cape of the oceans
Are all my heart and soul

Truthfully, the real secret of secrets is your own heart.

Sheng-yen Lu

34. Secret of Secrets

I remember, when I was young, I discovered a bomb shelter behind my home. The bomb shelter was at an off path location, so it became my secret hiding place - my secret fortress all through my childhood.

GaiGai!

When I was a child and when I was hurt, felt wronged or unhappy, failed a test, bullied by my classmate, or scolded by my teacher or parents, I hid in the bomb shelter. Sitting quietly, sometimes tearing up and sometimes sighing. In the darkness of the bomb shelter, my sorrows and worries gradually settled.

By the time I was ready to come out, my mood had totally changed. My eyes became brighter and my heart became lighter as I stepped out from the bomb shelter.

Actually, I did nothing in the secret bomb shelter and of course could not do anything anyway. I only went into the darkness of the bomb shelter to calm down and be away from other people. Just like this, in seclusion, all my injuries healed.

Now, I am an adult. For nine years I went into seclusion so I could cultivate. There are three years at Ling Xian Pavillion, six years in Tahiti, Taiwan, and Seattle.

Where I was during my seclusion was kept a secret, so I would not be disturbed. With a simple life, a pure heart, and at a secret place, I was able to get in touch with my inner self.

GaiGai!

Truthfully, the real secret of secrets is your own heart. To tell your heart, all that is private, all complaints, and secrets you know of. This is a communication with one's own heart.

I may go to an empty valley.

Or to a river.

Or to a desert.

Or to a forest.

Or to the top of a skyscraper

Or to the beach.

I will call out to the empty space and the stars, "GaiGai!"

I want to talk about my loneliness.

Talk about my silence.

Talk about my helplessness.

Talk about my attainments from many years of cultivation.

After many times of practice and purifications like this, my spirit renewed with more dharma taste. Sweet, elegant, refreshment, and joy continue to come alive.

I have given you the secret of secrets. Now my secrets are your secrets. They are not just about the present, but also include the Moon River with all the lovely images. Let our lives become more interesting.

Poem:

Everyone has secrets in their heart
These secrets have their own meanings
It's a pity that it may not be revealed
Let me write it in a sonnet

A sonnet written for you
Hope you will listen to
Your heart's rhythm
Your heart's rhyme
The eternal rhythm and rhyme of secrets

What cannot be said
And what is hard to tell
Can only be expressed
In an abstract painting
This warm spring-like happiness
Is the secret imprint of secrets

During those peaceful days there were no intrusions of triviality nor entanglements of any sorts that penetrated into my heart. It was just pure emptiness.

Sheng-yen Lu

35. Sincere Gratitude

GaiGai! I am grateful to be able to find you in this hectic world. I am grateful and very thankful.

To me, I am just a cultivator, a founder of a religious school of five million students. This is definitely a good thing, but I feel the cold and the loneliness being at the top.

I can only be near nature. Watching the clouds change its forms. Feeling the changing seasons as the flowers bloom and wilt.

I must cultivate daily to receive the dharma taste and my writings let me express these thoughts. My books are like pearls emitting lights of diamonds.

I find myself in deep thought when I take a walk by myself. Enjoying the rain, enjoying the fog, enjoying the snow, enjoying the moon, enjoying the flowers, enjoying the grass, or the creek, or the trees, and also the squirrels jumping from tree to tree.

My conversations are only with "Golden Mother of the Jade Pond," "Amitabha," "Ksitigarbha Bodhisattva," and other buddhas and bodhisattvas.

My prayers and supplications had all been heard by the buddhas and bodhisattvas. All the buddhas and bodhisattvas have reciprocated. All these surpassed ordinary conversations. For this is the heart to heart communication.

Every day passes peacefully, and thus continues for many years - many many good years.

I am very thankful for this!

GaiGai!

During those peaceful days there were no intrusions of triviality nor entanglements of any sorts that penetrated into my heart. It was just pure emptiness.

At this time, you appeared!

Very quickly you became my intimate friend. You have a beautiful voice with a lovely tone. I love to hear you sing. You have the "right view." You are a good analyst and a talented artist. All is clear. You have not created more worries for me, but instead gave me an inner peace. This is life. What more can I ask for?

I enjoy:

> Flowers in full bloom.
> Trees tall and straight.
> Grass on the wild prairie.
> Water ripples.
> And GaiGai, my lover's image, the refreshing fragrance, the enchanted atmosphere, abundance of wisdom and full of joy.
> All the problems in the troubled human world can be resolved.

I am very thankful and feel deeply grateful. I respectfully bow to the White Dakini. Thank the vast sky for the teachings. This *Remembrance of the Moon River* will extend limitlessly to the great earth.

I am lost for words. To GaiGai, the White Dakini, nothing but gratitude, and more gratitude.

How can I thank you? How could I express this? You appeared due to my persistent cultivation and my diligent book writing.

All in all----
The world became a more beautiful and perfect place.

Poem:

My grateful heart has already taken flight
My thankfulness is only a short message in the vast open sky.

There is nothing that can fully express my thankfulness
For different is different
I do not like the wording on ordinary cards
Which are all the same
How can it be the same for the most valuable
Nothing can compare
For there is nothing that is comparable
The next chapter in my life
Will be full of hope

I understand that meetings and scatterings will never end and also the cycle of happiness and sadness will be continuous.

Sheng-yen Lu

36. Let's Fly up to the Sky

I discovered that happiness and sadness are cyclical. I also discovered that the cycle of meetings and departures never stop.
Once a group of disciples sang a song for me:
Grand Master Ah!
Do you know
How much we love you?
We want to fly up with you to the blue sky.
....
Not realizing, my heart flew up like flying together in the blue sky. But, then I realized that it is just a song. For flying up to the blue sky is just a dream.
GaiGai!
You also know this song "Fly up Together into the Blue Sky." You are the White Dakini. So, of course you can fly up to the sky. I am Padmakumara. So, of course, I can also fly up to the sky. But, how about the holy disciples?
Usually this is of no concern. But, I have made a vow to bring all my disciples up to the blue sky. That is why, I have not forgotten, I shall not forsake any sentient being.

Therefore, I must wait till every sentient being is able to fly up to the blue sky, before I fly up to the blue sky, for this is the vow I made.

How much time would this take? I cannot forget that I have this important responsibility that would take innumerable human lifetimes. I cannot just pick up and leave or fly away just because I feel like it.

So GaiGai! The White Dakini! We can fly up together into the blue sky, but I cannot stay there. I must return to the human world to deliver all of them.

You should not think that I like to roam like the water at the Moon River. My heart has not hardened. I am still me. Only because, I understand that meetings and scatterings will never end and also the cycle of happiness and sadness will be continuous.

You must forgive me.

You must understand me.

You must encourage me.

Let me continue to deliver sentient beings! I wish to have unlimited burning lamps. Will you help me grow?

GiaGai!

If you really want to help me, it is really important, that you meet up with me for all our lifetimes.

I now understand:

It is not flying together up to the blue sky, but lifetimes of togetherness.

The Western Pureland of Ultimate Bliss.

The Maha Twin Lotus Pond.

Scenic site by the River of Heaven.

I cannot decide whether to go back or not. GaiGai! What do you say? It is not important to me now.

The only important thing is: YOU.

Let me write a poem then!

Roaming is coming and going
But coming and going has lost its meaning
We are constantly in the waves of life
Vows cannot be forsaken

You and me fly up together into the sky
Away from the games of human world
In this way
We can forget for a while

There is a major decision to make
To pick up
To give up
But the vow of my bodhicitta
Cannot change
Cannot be discarded
It is the melody forever

I tried to provide for my father's needs, the best way I could, as is the responsibility of a son.

Sheng-yen Lu

37. Pay Respect to My Father

GaiGai! Listen to me. My regards for my father are polarized. When I was a child, for many reasons, my father viewed me with disdain.

So I never called out to "dad" once before high school. I only knew to call out to "mom."

My father often beat me. A big beating every three days and a small beating every two days. The beatings continued even when the "wooden sword" broke.

My father often scolded me and for no reason, just get mad.

My mom was unable to help me because she was dominated by my dad too.

I ran away often, but was dragged back and got another hurtful beating.

That was my childhood.

My childhood sufferings, could this be child abuse? I do not know. Would this be domestic violence? I do not know.

My suffering from disdain, beatings, scolding, and unequal treatment was caused by the circumstances surrounding my birth, which was later revealed to me by my aunt.

And yet, because of my father's abuse, I received empowerment. I became:

1. Independent
2. Progressive
3. Confident
4. Decisive
5. Courageous

My spirit of forging ahead and perseverance comes from the empowerments from my dad.

This is why I pay respect to my dad.

***

GaiGai!

My father got older and was physically weaker, then my mom died. I began to feel empathy for my father, a lonely old man without anyone to depend on. He told me, "There is no more enjoyment left, but to eat."

I taught him the Buddhadharma, and he became a believer and a faithful cultivator.

My father took refuge in me.

My father also became a Buddhist disciple. He attended every dharma talk and received every empowerment from me.

He was wheelchair bound for a year and couldn't walk anymore. But after my empowerment, he was able to stand up and walk again.

I hired a caregiver for my father and took up the responsibility of caring for his daily life and expenses.

I tried to provide for my father's needs, the best way I could, as is the responsibility of a son.

I pay my respect to my father.

My father believing in Buddha and reciting the Buddha's name is more than enough for me.

Most respectful was my father's happy open laugh in his old age! This is most satisfying for us, as his daughters and son!

Poem:

> *Go deeply into one's own heart*
> *Listen to one's true voice*
> *Softly, softly*
> *The remembrance of the Moon River*
>
> *Listen closely*
> *One should not have hate*
> *Whatever happened*
> *Is due to causes of many many lifetimes*
>
> *Even of fallen leaves*
> *Even of blooming flowers*
> *Even of the soft blowing of the breeze*
> *If one can come to understand*
> *Clearer, and clearer Buddha's teachings*
> *As in "The Filial Piety Sutra"*

My self nature is pure and I understand that misunderstandings happen, but I am empty and non-existing, so I do not get upset.

Sheng-yen Lu

38. Even Misunderstandings Do Not Remain

GaiGai! You asked, "Was the Buddha upset when people misunderstood and thought that he caused Cinca-Manavika, a Brahmin woman, to become pregnant; when people thought he was intimate with Sundari; when Devadatta misunderstood and deserted the Buddha and took a group of disciples."

I answered, "No."

A reporter from Apple Magazine asked, "Grand Master Lu, do you get upset when you face negative publicity and are misunderstood?"

I answered, "No."

I have two explanations to misunderstandings:

The first one:

Misunderstandings happen so often in this world. No one really understands anyone. So much so that no one can truly understand themselves. At times, one can feel confused with oneself.

Even for the most intimate couples, misunderstandings happen.

Most people know me through media reports and tainted reports cause people to misunderstand me. Therefore, I say being misunderstood is normal.

Misunderstandings happen equally to everyone, then there is no need to feel hurt and it is justified to have a clear conscience.

The second is:

The Buddha reached enlightenment and attained self realization, the ultimate righteousness of equanimity. Self pureness supersedes normal man and holy beings.

The Buddha is beyond normal. Misunderstandings are normal. There is no need to be upset.

I am Grand Master Lu and I am also enlightened and attained self realization with no birth and dharma tolerance, ultimate knowledge of righteousness. My self nature is pure and I understand that misunderstandings happen, but I am empty and non-existing, so I do not get upset.

Misunderstandings will not affect me because misunderstandings will not stay - don't even need to shrug it off. Others thought it is a misunderstanding, but this is natural. There is no need to be hurtful or upset!

GaiGai!

Misunderstandings can upset ordinary people.

Misunderstandings can be hurtful. You will suffer from the ups and downs of the waves in your life.

Most people view misunderstandings as a big wave. Cultivators must learn to surf it. Experience the process of surfing to find the enjoyment of surfing and overcoming the big wave brings the joy of satisfaction.

"Obstacles."

"Oppressions."

"Slandering."

"Hatred."

It's all the same.

And yet, to me these do not stay. I do not take these to heart, therefore they will not affect me.

GaiGai! This is why I do not suffer!

Poem:

It is natural for leaves to fall
Destiny is written on the dry fallen leaves
Don't feel sad for autumn
This is the way for seasons to celebrate life

Misunderstandings happen to everyone the same
Who understands who in this world
If this is so
Then why bother to complain about this

It is not necessary to make a point to explain
Misunderstandings come
Misunderstandings go
This is just human nature
Only the enlightened and self realized
Will truly know

Come naturally and go naturally. Don't be obstinate. In this way, will reduce troubles and worries and obtain release!

Sheng-yen Lu

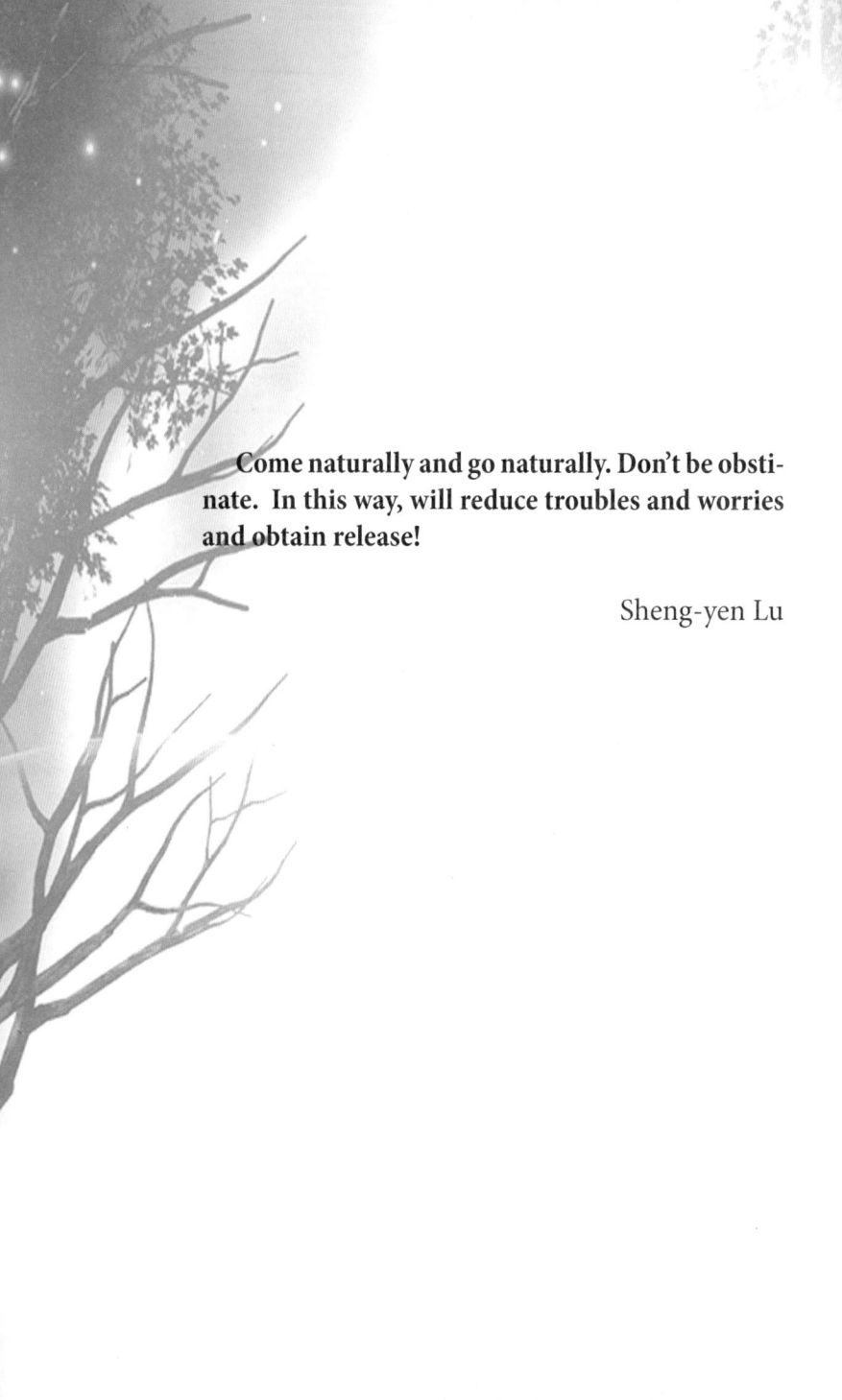

39. Self Imposed Restrictions

Remember the conversation with a Zen master? Someone said to the Zen master, "My heart is not at peace."
The Zen master replied, "Give me your heart and I will take it to peace."
Someone said to the Zen master, "I want to be released!"
The Zen master asked, "Who tied you down?"
This conversation is simple, but powerful. Its meaning is deep and causes one to reflect. The reason one is not at peace is oneself. The reason one cannot feel free is self bondage. These days many people are bounded by themselves.
One word to describe sentient beings is "lost."
One word to describe the Buddha is "enlightenment."
Human emotions are complicated and confusing. Human pursuits are complicated and confusing. Human life is due to the word "lost." Lost in pursuits of fame, money, beauty, food, and sleep.
Many people are lost in desires of "wealth."
Many people are lost in desires of "appearance."
Many people are lost in desires of "position."
Often they are in pursuit for lifetime after lifetime and can never

come out of the maze of desires. Sometimes there is an abrupt awakening, but they re-enter the maze of desires again.

My personal opinion is:

In the pursuit of money, beauty, fame, food and sleep, just let it come and go by itself. It is best to just let it happen naturally.

To have is good.

To not have is good.

Come naturally and go naturally. Don't be obstinate. In this way, will reduce troubles and worries and obtain release!

The Buddha taught us:

Rid of self.

Rid of the way.

This the path.

GaiGai!

Life is like a big pot of dye. Most of the people are submerged in it. Sentient beings are deeply lost in it. Not many people can get out of it. This is why they are not free.

GaiGai!

Sometimes I feel like I cannot go on. When I really can't go on, I will leave and find another stage. If I really can't go on here, I will leave again and find another stage.

Once again, if I can't go on and there is no other place to go then I will go into recluse! Might as well be alone and let me have my freedom.

I believe when this time comes you will be by my side, not in form, always guarding over me.

Poem:

Pursuit
Of wanting everything
Wanting this, wanting that, want, want, want, want, want
Then
Worry, worry, worry, worry, worry
Like the lifetime struggling sound of the cicada
The cicada's sound is uncountable
The cidada's sound is not laughter

The Buddha said
Nothing tangible, nothing tangible, nothing tangible
Having is also the same as not having
This is the remedy for pureness
But the lost souls
Inescapable, inescapable, inescapable

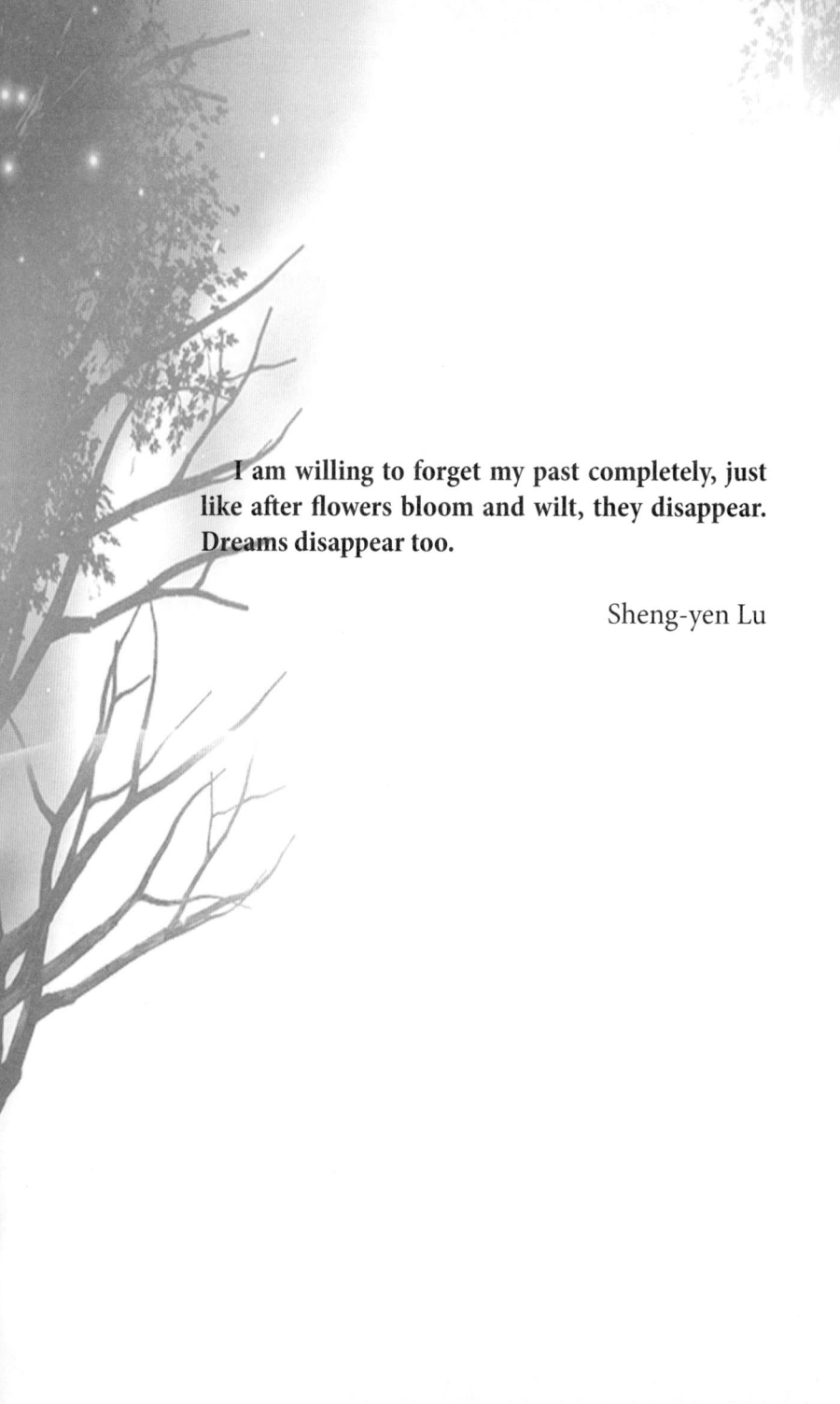

I am willing to forget my past completely, just like after flowers bloom and wilt, they disappear. Dreams disappear too.

Sheng-yen Lu

40. Is GaiGai the White Dakini?

Reading this book up to this point, some people claim: "GaiGai! She is the White Dakini! Validated. Can't be wrong!"

I did not deny the reader's statement, but I did not nod my head in acknowledgment either. Just let them talk about it!

I can only say the following:

Sometimes GaiGai is in front of me.

Sometimes GaiGai is as far away as the other side of the sky.

Anyway, GaiGai is like a lamp or like a moon hanging in space.

A lamp will emit light.

The moon can also radiate light.

GaiGai's brightness lights up this traveler's heart, reflecting wisdom.

GaiGai will appear during my most sorrowful moment to wipe away my tears.

GaiGai will console me when I am really feeling down, to enliven me again.

When I feel life can't go on anymore, GaiGai appears to be my pillar of life.

GaiGai truly fills my heart till it overflows.

I am very thankful whether for the lamp in front of me or the moon far up in the sky. We are merged into one. Merging irrespective of distance.

Even if we are apart, I only have to think of GaiGai. No matter day or night, GaiGai will appear in front of me, silently smiling with radiance.

I am writing this book *Remembrance of Moon River* to show my respect and gratitude.

Because of the cause and effect of the "remembrance of the Moon River," as well as our deep affinity due to the "remembrance of the Moon River" keep us tightly together.

GaiGai!

You have already made a deep imprint on my heart in this life. I have also made a deep imprint on your heart. This imprint will create a scar that will be with us in our next life and will never disappear.

I am willing to forget my past completely, just like after flowers bloom and wilt, they disappear. Dreams disappear too. But I cherish the remembrance of the Moon River. They will never wilt like flowers.

The inspiration keeps coming like the remembrance of the Moon River. For now, it is very valuable.

GaiGai! I know you were looking for me.

GaiGai! You also know that I was looking for you.

GaiGai! Some say you are the White Dakini. I however, did not acknowledge or deny it. This is our secret.

Long Live! Long Live!

The dharma body of the White Dakini.

The bliss body of the White Dakini.

The emanation body of the White Dakini.

Poem:

You have combined both worlds
Like the rainbow
Imagery has color and form
I can only remain silent

Take refuge in White Dakini
The response from merging
I made a vow
The vow that I made
Is nailed with steel
It is not made in jest
Nor is it a lie
A real promise

I feel that the continuation of a religion needs various empowerments. Not only the empowerments of the buddhas, bodhisattvas, and root gurus, but also the leaders of the country.

Sheng-yen Lu

41. A Letter from President Obama

GaiGa! A few days ago, President Obama sent me a letter co-signed by Michelle Obama.

While I was spreading the dharma in Taiwan, Dr. Fo-ching Lu, my daughter, opened the letter and informed me about it.

There are letters given to me from three American presidents: former President Ronald Reagan, former President Bill Clinton, and President Barack Obama.

During his term in office, I corresponded with President Clinton and received the most letters from him.

Gary Faye Locke, the Secretary of Commerce, a member of President Obama's cabinet, is an old acquaintance of mine. We have known each other since he ran for Governor of Washington. Mutual affirmation caused our affinity.

I never corresponded with President Bush. The reason is because Dr. Fo-ching Lu is a Democrat and President Bush was a Republican.

I, however am an independent.

GaiGai!

The letters from the American presidents are mostly words of encouragement.

A country's president thanking and encouraging his citizens is enough.

Of course, the encouragement from the president is very important.

This is an "opportunity."

I came from Taiwan and settled in America. I founded True Buddha School, which is worldwide. True Buddha School settled, grew and came to fruition.

I feel that the continuation of a religion needs various empowerments. Not only the empowerments of the buddhas, bodhisattvas, and root gurus, but also the leaders of the country.

When everything is in place True Buddha School blooms naturally. GaiGai!

Our True Buddha School has the empowerment from the White Dakini like the published book *The Sword of the Yogi* is an empowerment from you to establish a clear system for spreading the dharma.

The instructions are very clear on the methods of cultivation.

You clarified:

The importance of precepts.

The importance of tolerance.

Every mistake and transgression expounded.

What is desolate cold?

What is abundant warmth?

What are the three lower realms?

GaiGai! You taught all the disciples to cultivate towards the warmth and avoid the cold desolation.

The Sword of the Yogi taught us the proper way of cultivation and at the same time to avoid the tragic death and, most importantly, to avoid descending to the three lower realms and return to pureness.

GaiGai!

You have made the True Buddha School more perfect!

Poem:

Our needs are all fulfilled
We have delivered and accepted both cold and warm sentient beings
The noble
The humble
All are fulfilled with your grace
We encourage people to stay away from the hazardous path
Shake off the worldly dust from our body
Increase brightness daily

With taste of true passion
It is not necessary to bow respectfully, humbly
On the ascending road of cultivation
Going up step by step

I will not change, or be upset, definitely never put pressure on things, or need to appease.

Sheng-yen Lu

42. Disciples are Also Like Water

GaiGai! I often say, "Come and go according to affinity." This is why I am not distressed when disciples leave.

I said, "Disciples are like water. They flow in and flow away." I have said this before, which is actually the way it is.

I also said, "What I don't like most is you leaving me!"

You answered, "I will not!"

I know you won't, because we have vows over lifetimes. Vows of the space are vows of no endings. Vows that draw us closer even if we are far apart.

We all hope that we will be well liked by everyone. As the founder of a Buddhist school, I have the same hope, but I know: the more affinity there is, the closer the relationship.

Whereas if there is no affinity, the disciple will leave.

This is how it is and has not changed for centuries. Coercion will not work. Coercion will not be natural. So I take it as is, with ease. This is why it does not bother me when disciples leave, for disciples are like water.

This is why I don't try to appease others or censor myself and am always frank and never speculate about what is on my disciples' mind.

I have never put on an air as the founder of a religious school. All I have is a pure open heart.

Truthfully, I always go with the flow of affinity and never put pressure on anything. I have this kind of mentality because early on I authenticated that "affinities are due to cause and effect." I will not change, or be upset, definitely never put pressure on things, or need to appease.

There is no need for sadness, worry, sighs, or anger.

Because this is all the way of nature.

All actions are impermanent, so disciples flow like water.

There is no "me" in any dharma, so disciples flow like water.

Nirvana is a quiet peace, so disciples flow like water.

(You must contemplate these three verses.)

It is fine to go and come back or wander in and out because I will not forsake any sentient beings.

But I will always remember that: like a dream, like a mirage, like bubbles, like shadows, waves are not forever, rainbows are not forever, human life is not forever. Nothing is real. Everything is an illusion!

However, I do want you, White Dakini to hold my hand and mind and not let go. Leaving your imprint in my heart.

GaiGai!

I will always remember your words:

"I never will!"

Poem:

I saw patches of clouds in the sky
I saw rolling waves in the ocean
Vast oceans turning to rich fields
I know people's mind are full of ideas

I know relationships between people are due to affinity
I know seasons will change from spring, summer, fall
And winter
Although there is a procedure
Still swinging back and forth like a swing

I understand, understand, understand
Within the clearness are some unclearness
Still hoping
The everlasting vows
Is my endless journey

Not realizing that they are lost, unable to come out of darkness, as well as unable to determine illusions, will cause the continuous cycle of reincarnation within the six realms.

Sheng-yen Lu

43. Self Authenticated Buddha-nature

Whenever I go through a tunnel I think how this is much like "life."

When we come near the end of the long tunnel, the white light shoots in from the end. The appearance of the beautiful bright light reminds me of the appearance of the Buddha-nature.

Frankly, if "self authenticated Buddha-nature" counts as success then of the many successes in my life, the most successful is not establishing the True Buddha School, or having five million disciples, or of writing hundreds of books, or of spreading the dharma for a few decades, or of the delivering of spirits, but rather the only real success in my life is "self authenticated Buddha-nature."

In my experience this world has many "people" and "birds" that fly in the sky, "animals" that crawl or walk on earth, and "fish" that swim in water. They are all categorized as sentient beings.

Then there are also:

"Kinnaras (human-like non-humans)."
"Ghosts."
"Gods."
"Spirits."

"Star bodies."

"Heavenly beings."

These are sentient beings as well. The category of "sentient beings" is very wide.

Now, I am going to tell you all. These "sentient beings" all abide in the dark tunnels of the human world. From birth to death they stay in the dark tunnels.

Why?

This is how I see it. Aside from "self authenticated Buddha-nature," all sentient beings are lost in darkness and illusions.

Not realizing that they are lost, unable to come out of darkness, as well as unable to determine illusions, will cause the continuous cycle of reincarnation within the six realms.

GaiGai!

Even individuals who have an abundance of wealth are still lost. Even with the highest title, they are still lost. Even with beauty, they are still lost.

These things do not count. In Buddha's eyes, these are not successes, and they are lost, lost, lost.

GaiGai!

You are the "White Dakini."

You came down from the scenic site of the Heavenly River, so naturally you would understand me. When you are with me, you always have a beautiful smile for me.

When you are not by my side, I miss you deeply. There are no demands or complaints between you and me.

Yes, we both attained enlightenment and realized Buddha-nature. We both self authenticated our Buddha-nature. We both arrived at the Western Pureland. We both authenticated bliss.

Only because the body is still in the human world, but the heart has already surpassed.

Poem:

The heart is forever oscillating in space
Quietly studying the image of the mountains
And the twisting of the river
Admiring the picturesque sunset

Already an old cultivator
Not because of loneliness
Not because of depressed emotions
Can only hear the drums of dawn and the morning bells

Understand emptiness
A brief feeling of beauty
Like entering into the empty tunnel
Like blowing bubbles
And popping
What is North, South, West, and East

Every chapter has a point. Read it this way and the conflicting characters will not cause boredom.

Sheng-yen Lu

44. The Feeling of Confusion

Up to this point there seems to be some confusion that there are three GaiGai.

The first GaiGai seems to be a human, cared by Grand Master Lu.

The second GaiGai seems to be from heaven. A heavenly being who has been with Grand Master Lu

The third GaiGai seems to be the White Dakini, who is here to teach and direct Grand Master Lu.

These three differences were confusing in this book and even caused me to be confused.

I wrote the book this way for a reason. I want readers to understand my bodhisattva feelings and disregard whether what is "true" or "false" and not pursue GaiGai's identity.

I wish:

Readers will read this book with dark spectacles, not study it in depth, but to admire the flower in the fog. Enjoy the flowers' special beauty in the moonlight; enjoy the adorable romantic words and the sincere frankness of the characters.

If we apply the three bodies of Buddhism to them, then the three GaiGai characters are not contradictory:

The White Dakini is the dharma body (Dharmakaya).
The heavenly GaiGai is the enjoyment body (Sambhogakaya).
The human GaiGai is the manifestation body (Nirmanakaya).

Anyway, you must feel this book is Grand Master Lu professing his love, and the whole world would instantly brighten up. Each short essay is independent and has its own point. Read it this way and you would not be turned away by the paradoxes.

I often tell people:

People must be complementary to each other, heavenly beings, and White Dakini. Mutual respect for each other will begin a perfect friendship.

I hope everyone will have a broad mind. For this will bring happiness.

However, if one has a narrow mind then this book may cause many distresses.

Don't close your mind. The mind must be open to take in Grand Master Lu's loving narratives and dialogue.

Someone asked, "Grand Master Lu is sixty six years old. Can there be more love narrations?"

I answered, "My whole life I have been innocently romantic and at sixty six years old, I am still innocently romantic."

GaiGai said, "Grand Master Lu is innocently romantic because of his candidness."

I said, "Because of this, I feel I am always surrounded by the beauty of flowers, the radiance of flowers, the fragrance of flowers, and a lot of other stories related to flowers."

Don't mind whether the characters are real or not.

What is real is Grand Master Lu's sincere romantic narrations.

Poem:

A flower bloomed in the Garden of Poems in my heart
As my eyes followed
Becoming sweeter and sweeter

As if the flower turned to spirit
Fermenting the honey wine of emotions
Infusing fragrance

Please listen quietly to the sincere words from my heart
Saying so many promises
From year to year

Affinities rise and ebb in front of our eyes
Like an illusion
Of a rainbow
But, at that very moment
How poetic is the heart

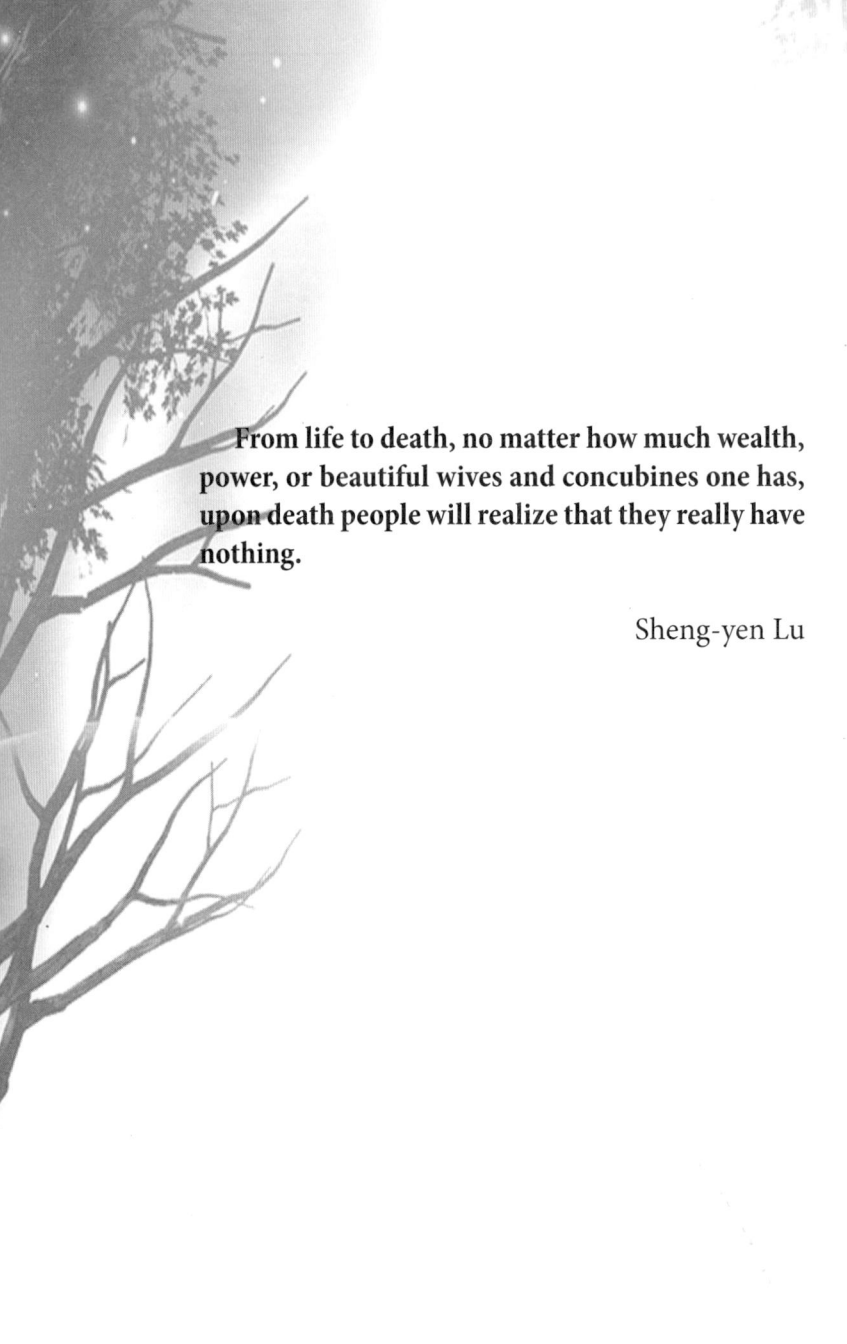

From life to death, no matter how much wealth, power, or beautiful wives and concubines one has, upon death people will realize that they really have nothing.

Sheng-yen Lu

45. As an Illusion or As a Dream

When I was in Hong Kong, I met Abbott Guoxian of the Hui-Quan Temple. We exchanged our views of "enlightenment and authentication of buddha-nature."

Abbott Guoxian said to me, "Ah! So illusionary feelings arise from illusions!"

I said, "Only Buddha-nature escapes reincarnation!"

GaiGai!

You have said, "Feels like a dream, until now, it felt like one dream after another. I often ask myself if this is another dream!"

Let me tell you the truth:

This universe is a big dream. This world is a medium size dream. Our surroundings are a small dream. Our individual life is a tiny, tiny dream.

When we dream at night, we only know that this is a dream upon awakening.

When we awaken from a good or bad dream, we realize that it is only a dream. Unexpectedly laughing or crying, either letting it go or holding on to it.

The Buddha told us that the hundred years of human life is a hundred year dream.

From life to death, no matter how much wealth, power, or beautiful wives and concubines one has, upon death people will realize that they really have nothing. A hundred years is also a dream.

"A lifetime's dream in the time span of cooking rice" - is it not a dream too?

People view this world to be real. What we see and what we hear are all real. They only realize that this is a dream when death arrives. All is empty.

The Buddha meant to say:

The world around you seems real, but it really is only an illusion.

Rain----water----ice----vapor----cloud.

Flower----wilt----wither----dust----mud.

Infant----child----adolescent----adult----old age.

See!

Everyone and everything is like this. Every stage is like a mini-dream. As each stage passes, there is no turning back.

The Buddha said, "The mind knows the illusion and not minding it is the cultivation of mindlessness."

Nothing to gain.

Nothing to mind.

Nothing to dwell.

So, like this, all sufferings will naturally disappear. Then this is not far from reaching enlightenment!

Poem:

The remembrance of the Moon River
Forever roaming
Travelers with the backpack
Going from stop to stop

Follow the crowd, follow the scene
Big cities and countryside
The train on the rails
Clickity clack, clickity clack

Guarantee you will never be able to visit all
The scenic sites in this lifetime
They are only the dream illusions from ancient to modern

You said, "All these are temporary. They are like the illusions in the dream, obstacles of your own doing. You only need to have faith and cultivate diligently to arise above it."

Sheng-yen Lu

46. Surpass Obstacles After Obstacles

When I was young, I was in many predicaments. My antecedent was questioned from the time of my birth.

Growing up, I experienced many indescribable and unmentionable sufferings. If I wasn't adaptable, I would have been dead long ago.

I was not very studious in my youth and was held back two times, transferred from school to school and also dealing with the obstacles of learning.

Because I had no money for college, I was not able to take the national college exams and continue my education in a regular college, but had to go to the military academy. This was the obstacle of my college education.

During my military days, I was also learning about religion. Because of the special conditions of military life, there were times when I felt like I was walking the edge of deep cliffs.

Stop and go, stop and go, taking each step carefully to avoid any traps or points of no return.

The Surveyor Chief said, "Don't be superstitious. Stop this right away."

The Security Chief said, "You have been under surveillance for five years."

The Inspector Officer said, "I have to write a report daily on you."

The Chief of Police said, "Investigate Sheng-yen Lu."

Sometimes, it felt like I was stuck in a crevice unable to retreat and unable to advance.

After stepping out into society, I discovered the blows thrown at me from the slanderous comments of other Buddhist schools.

Blows from the public.

Blows from public commentators.

Blows from the media.

Misunderstandings here and misunderstandings there. I was trapped deeply in the dark tunnel of endless negative reports, which affected my reputation with the government. It became difficult to clear my name.

In this lifetime, obstacle after obstacle kept hitting me like big waves in the storm, where the second wave comes in before the first wave subsides.

***

The White Dakini said:

Your feelings are rained upon under a dark cloud. You feel no peace, corralled in the corner and unable to expand.

Misunderstandings, false, and slanderous comments are all blows which wiped out all the effort you put in.

Depression set in.

The heart became deathly cold.

Became unsociable.

GaiGai!

You said, "All these are temporary. They are like the illusions in the dream, obstacles of your own doing. You only need to have faith and cultivate diligently to arise above it."

GaiGai said, "The weather is impermanent. The storm will pass, windy waves will pass. So shall everything else."
GaiGai said, "Everything goes in cycles!"
What GaiGai said "everything is cyclic," is very true!

Poem:

> *It seems the storm never ends*
> *Seattle's rain continues to rain in my heart*
> *Sunshine has to shine sometime*
> *In a clear blue sky*
>
> *I have already accomplished mindlessness*
> *Storms will not influence me*
> *Heavy clouds*
> *Thunderous rain*
> *Will only be a moment*
> *Soon clear skies will remove all darkness*

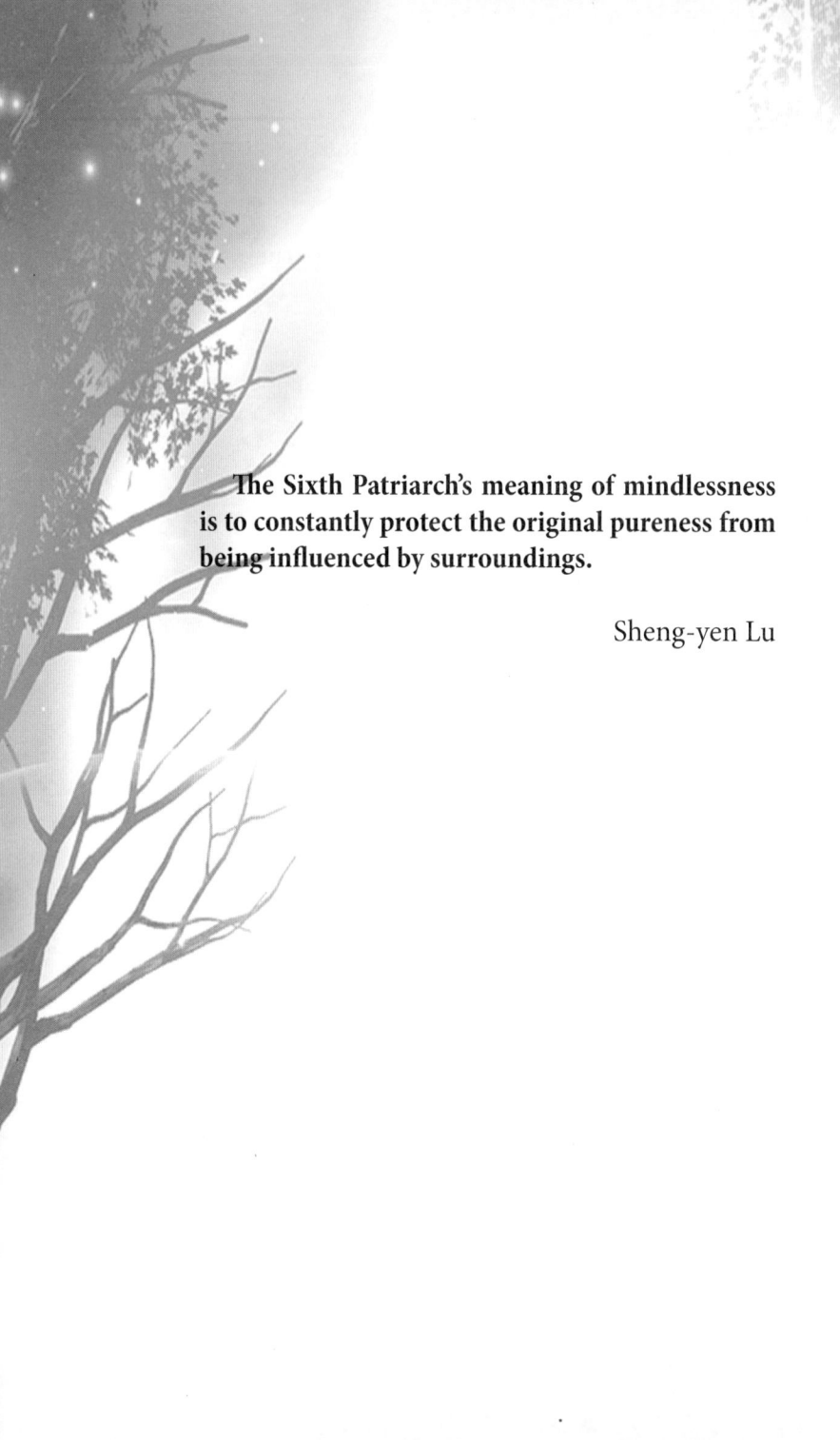

The Sixth Patriarch's meaning of mindlessness is to constantly protect the original pureness from being influenced by surroundings.

Sheng-yen Lu

47. Dharma Talks About the Sixth Patriarch

My recent Dharma Talks expounded on the *Platform Sutra of the Sixth Patriarch*. The Sixth Patriarch Huineng was a grand Zen Master who shined a different light.

Some people think Zen Buddhists teach meditation.

Some people think that meditation is about sitting quietly and not thinking about anything. When no thought arises is when one authenticates one's own Buddha-nature.

Most cultivators think that thousands of thoughts become one thought.

One thought becomes no thought.

No thought is the fruition of Buddhahood.

But, the Sixth Patriarch Huineng said this is wrong.

The Sixth Patriarch did not think that mindlessness is the same as emptiness or nothingness or bodiless, but rather thought is still present, only that it cannot be influenced by anything to affect its original pureness, and this is what the Sixth Patriarch believed mindlessness is.

Deep meditation means that the mind is not being affected by its surroundings to alter its pure origin.

The Sixth Patriarch gave an example. He said that Vimalakirti once reprimanded Sariputra for going into the forest to meditate for a long time. For this, Vimalakirti said Sariputra did not understand meditation.

For the Sixth Patriarch, entering into samadhi is meditation and coming out of samadhi is also meditation. Deep meditation is meditation in daily lives. The Sixth Patriarch's meaning of mindlessness is to constantly protect the original pureness from being influenced by surroundings.

The Sixth Patriarch emphasized:

"To have no thoughts during meditation is a big mistake."

"You can still have thoughts, but mindlessness occurs when the mind is not influenced."

It is difficult for cultivators to differentiate between these two sayings. I reached enlightenment and authenticated my self Buddha-nature when I was able to fully distinguish and understand these two sayings.

GaiGai!

Normally cultivators are told to meditate by sitting quietly and relaxing one's mind and body.

Eyes observe the nose, the nose observes the heart, gather attention on deep, slow, long, quiet breaths and slowly close the eyes.

When thoughts and attention gather then there will be a response.

Reflecting on the thoughts, and the mind, then suddenly entering into meditation. Then dharma empowerment enters the top of the head, light appears, enter the emptiness of the First Dhyana Heaven where body and mind is empty.

Practice meditation this way daily and receive the dharma taste of joy and peace.

GaiGai!

I personally feel that utilizing this method to achieve peace, dharma taste, dharma enjoyment, dharma empowerment, emptiness, and light - this is all good.

But one must remember the teachings of Cultivator Lu the Sixth Patriarch. [The Sixth Patriarch's last name is also Lu.]

Mindlessness does not mean no thought arises.

Mindlessness is not the emptiness of body and mind.

Rather, it is the heart and mind of the cultivator not being smudged, having no worries - self authenticated Buddha-nature is really mindlessness.

I feel this kind of meditation can only be achieved when one attains enlightenment and self authenticated Buddha-nature! Without reaching enlightenment and self authenticated Buddha-nature, mindlessness cannot be achieved.

Poem:

Send word to cultivators
Mindlessness is not without thoughts
Thoughts, thoughts, thoughts, thoughts
Not seeing is the real sight

The appearance of Buddha-nature
Is not meditation
Is not Dharma empowerment
Is not clear lights
It is forever the same

I have already let go of myself. I let go of my image. I let go of my surroundings, let go of my position, let go of my self pity, let go of other people's perception of me.

Sheng-yen Lu

48. Self Disappearance

Taiwan celebrates a lot of special days with special programs. The one that I look forward to most is the Children's Play Day in Yilan.

Frankly, when I observe myself, I notice that I am innocent, romantic, candid, and worst of all, naive.

I often act without thinking things through. I normally emphasize on positive thoughts and neglect to ponder the negatives.

Aye! I can't help the way I am.

GaiGai!

I often forget myself. I forget that I am now a monk. What I should do and what I shouldn't do. I don't remember that I am a monk until it is often too late.

This is the reason I enjoy Children's Play day.

Once, I was having fun swimming. I lost myself like a water droplet merging into the pool of water. I only realized how awful it was when I appeared in the news in my swimming gear.

Once, I lost myself while I was singing "Flower Woman." Not until I was, once again, criticized by the media did I begin only singing "college folk songs," which do not express the love between a man and a woman.

Once, I performed a dharma ceremony for gangsters. This was really naive and ridiculous.

Once, I let a gossip magazine interview me. This was being too candid.

Once, I wrote the book *Love Letters to a Monk* and thought it was romantic. Afterwards, I realized how naive it was.

....

All in all, I am like a child. Always unknowingly causing trouble.

Like today, I wrote *Remembrance of the Moon River*. Forgetting my age and writing something romantic. What will become of this? I could care less.

I have already let go of myself. I let go of my image. I let go of my surroundings, let go of my position, let go of my self pity, let go of other people's perception of me.

As though I'm reliving my childhood days, swimming in the little creek forgetting myself in the fun.

GaiGai!

Children's Play Day is so good!

I don't like to be an adult. I like to be a child.

Once, oh, who cares!

In the past, oh, who cares!

I know "naiveté," "romance," "candidness," and "innocence" are my faults. But, I will continue to be "naive," "romantic," "candid," and "innocent." Don't mention the past; don't mention the present; and don't even mention the future.

GaiGai!

I like the remembrance of the Moon River. So let it lightly, swiftly, unaffectedly, pace by!

Poem:

*I feel more and more like a child
My appearance has changed
But the mind does not know any better*

*Naive, naive, and still naive
As if nothing matters
The head is empty*

*Immersed in whatever I do
Because I put my mind into it
I don't even know why my heartbeat quickens
GaiGai
I really do not know
I really do not know what this is about*

One moment of negligence could cause severe damage. Then it will be difficult to have a "human body" again.

Sheng-yen Lu

49. Hurry to Lishan [Pear Mountain]

On August 19, 2010, I was invited to Dai Zang Temple at Lishan in Taiwan. Lishan is halfway up the Central Cross-Island Highway and is surrounded by approximately three thousand meters of mountains.

After the Jiji earthquake on September 21, 1999, several points on the Central Cross-Island Highway were impassable. A group of us started from Fengyuan, Dongshi, Tianleng, Guguan, Heping, and finally arrived at Lishan.

There were patrol stations on this stretch of the highway.

It took three and a half hours to cover this distance by car.

Seeing the damages on the highway, I was horrified by the disastrous effects of the big earthquake.

Shocked that the big boulder fell from the top.

Shocked that the big bridge broke into four sections.

Shocked that the rocks and mudslides that cut the mountain in half.

Shocked that the roadway sank half-way below.

Shocked that there were piles of falling rocks.

Shocked that there were streams of water rushing onto the road.

Shocked at seeing cars being driven into valleys of lakes.

During this rough rugged ride, a big rain storm came upon us as we approached Lishan.

I said, "I can't believe the Central Cross-Island Highway which was extremely well constructed, changed so drastically from Dongshi to Lishan."

How many years will it take to repair the destruction caused to the road?

Big earthquakes are horrifying!

GaiGai!

This is a metaphor of life.

We, practitioners, cultivating along on a regular leveled track.

Although it may be smooth, we still need to be careful and avoid mistakes.

If mistakes happen, such as losing faith, the imbalance could make us fall, as though we were falling from a cliff.

Upon awakening, we will find our body no longer exists.

GaiGai!

This apprehension is a cultivator's obstinate opinion. One big mistake can cause one to fall into a deep precipice.

Behind the obstinate opinion is the frightful steep cliff.

I told the dharma brothers and sisters of Dai Zang Temple:

To follow the Five Precepts.

To enact the Ten Virtuous Deeds.

To practice Six Paramitas.

I wish all my disciples will practice rectifying one's behavior, so cultivations will not be imperfect as imperfection may cause one to fall from the cliff, resulting in a broken body.

The trip to Mount Li reminded me that we have to be mindful of cultivation every second. One moment of negligence could cause severe damage. Then it will be difficult to have a "human body" again.

Poem:

Do not over reminisce on the glorious past
Time passed will not return
How can fallen leaves
Return to the tree

Do not over reminisce on the glorious past
The beauty of youth
And a slim body will not be forever
For by nature one will become old

Do not over reminisce on the glorious past
We need to realize the importance of now
Do not be lazy
Do not lose faith
Do not waste time on yesterday
Walk steadily on the heavenly bridge of "Right Dharma"

Only you can enter the depth of my heart and listen to my heart's voice. Wish we both have beautiful sweet dreams.

Sheng-yen Lu

50. Listening at the Wuling Farm

In the evening of August 19, 2010, after an hour of driving, we arrived at the Wuling Hoya Hotel. My room was number 313. Looking out from the french windows, I could see two mountains standing like a screen in front of my eyes with a creek, whose rapids were white and foamy, rushing towards the right.

The evening was black.

The mountains were black.

Only the water in the creek was white.

A few sparkles of light, around three to five, could be seen on the side of the mountain, but was quickly swallowed by the surrounding darkness.

It was a very calm night.

GaiGai!

I listened quietly.

The rushing creek water seemed to be singing my song. Quietly recounting the days of Moon River.

The ancient old secrets continuously revealed themselves.

The night breeze was cool.

It was humid and hot in the valley, the temperature was around thirty degrees Celsius. Yet, it was only sixteen degrees at Wuling Hoya. In my heart there was a melody. It was the melody of the song "Sky, Sky, Sky Blue" by Pan Yueyun :

> Sky, sky, sky blue
> It is hard not to think of him.
> Still the innocent child has to ask
> Why are your eyes sweating?
> Deep is the love,
> Full of emotions.
> Sufferings of separation.
> Thoughts are just emptiness.

Yes, it is getting closer and closer to autumn. The sonata of the falling leaves and gradual appearance of the autumn maple leaves created this calm quietness, bringing peace to my spirit. However, I am speechless because I don't know what else needs to be said to GaiGai. Wanting to say something and yet it seems as though nothing needs to be said. So we just stand by each other and remain in the song of speechlessness.

The earth has sounds of nature.

The mountains and rivers are naturally mysterious.

Please listen closely to the voices in my heart. It will reveal the reply from me to you.

***

GaiGai!

That night I slept sweetly.

When I woke up my first memory was nothing.

I turned my body and got out of bed.

I wrote this last article of *Remembrance of the Moon River*. Do you realize that what I want to tell you, you already know.

You are the best.

Only you can enter the depth of my heart and listen to my heart's voice. Wish we both have beautiful sweet dreams. Dreams to continue eternally. Let last night's sweetness continue every night!

Poem:

> *When tired of mundane trivial matters*
> *GaiGai*
> *Support is quietness*
>
> *When the heart is confused*
> *GaiGai*
> *Fright bursts like bubbles*
>
> *When ideas and thoughts get tangled*
> *GaiGai*
> *My head gets lighter*
> *(You brought me clear, relaxed happiness. Thank you for everything! The grand empowerment of the White Dakini)*

August 2010
Living Buddha Lian-sheng
Sheng-yen Lu
17102 NE 40th Ct
Redmond, WA
98052
U.S.A.

Appendix: A Gift of Wisdom (A Response from a Reader)

About Tai-Chi
Grand Master Lu asked his disciples three questions:
"Does Grand Master Lu really know the art of Tai-Chi?"
"Why does Grand Master Lu practice Tai-Chi?"
"Why does Grand Master Lu do the first time softly, the second time forcefully and the third time very forcefully?"
About practicing Tai-Chi, Grand Master Lu said:
"Expect surprising answers from my disciples and let old man Lu have a good laugh?"

***

For the first question:
"Does Grand Master Lu really know Tai-Chi?"
Disciple's answer:
Yin and yang are of the same family. It only takes a matchmaker to become one. Movement and stillness are one. To know or not to know

is a matter of two sides.

For the second question:
"Why does Grand Master Lu practice Tai-Chi?"
Disciple's answer:
No reason at all. Like passing water leaves no trace. Just because! Refreshing!

For the third question:
"Why does Grand Master Lu do the first time softly, the second time forcefully and the third time very forcefully?"
Disciple's answer:
Both gentleness and force should be used. The process is different, but the effect is the same. Passing through the body without a trace.
Don't talk nonsense, just practice for practice sake. Tai-Chi is none of your business. This is not a surprising answer, just hoping to get a laugh from Grand Master.
Ha, Ha, Ha! Sorry for the trouble! I'll pluck a hair and blow it towards space to make an offering to you Grand Master.

***

The Wilted Cherry Blossoms

Grand Master asked:
"The cherry blossoms blossomed, withered, and the season passed. In a Zen dialogue, how do you reply?"

***

Grand Master asked:
"Are cherry blossoms blossoming?"
Disciple's answer:

Let it happen naturally. How beautiful!
Spring comes and spring goes, flowers bloom and flowers wilt. This happens every year.
Grand Master asked:
"Wilted?"
Disciple's reply:
Let it be, let it fall!
Falling flowers and the passing of water. Is it coming or is it going?
Grand Master asked:
"Has the season passed?"
Disciple's reply:
It is none of my business!
Looking at the flowers in emptiness. Flowers are not flowers. Then what is there?
Left behind are the cherries! Here have one. It is just delicious!
The word delicious is something.

※※※

What Does Grand Master Lu Look Like?

Zen Master Yangshan asked:
"Do you see the monk that looks like a donkey?"
Zen Master Guangyong answered:
"I see the monk, but he does not look like a buddha."
Zen Master Yangshan asked:
"If not like a buddha, then what does he look like?"
Zen Master Guangyong answered:
"If he has to look like something, then what is the difference if he looks like a donkey?"
Grand Master Lu asked his disciples:
"What does Grand Master look like?"
Disciple's answer:

Difficult to describe what you look like or not look like. There is no people and there is no me.

There is a reason, but the reason is not clear. If there is no reason, then why reason? Grand Master Lu is Grand Master Lu. There is no need to look like anything. How can this be clarified?

Emergency - need to go to the bathroom - this is the real deal!

***

Front Three Three and Back Three Three

Grand Master Lu asked:
"How much is front three three and back three three?"
Disciple's answer:
Wind comes and wind leaves. Leaving no image or imprint. How much wind would you say?

Not too much, not too little, just enough, cool, cool, cool. Ha ha!

Just comfortable, not three or four. You are insulting people! Are you a person? Oh! This is it!

***

Eighty Million

Grand Master Lu said on the Dharma throne:
"Give everyone eighty million!"
[A "ten million" means "must take care to…" in Chinese.]

Ten million of happiness [must take care to have happiness]. Ten million of health [must take care to be healthy]. Ten million of exercises [must take care to exercise]. Ten million of no anger [must take care not to get angry]. Ten million of contentment [must take care to be content]. Ten million of good deeds [must take care to do good deeds]. Ten million of cultivations [must take care to cultivate].

Grand Master asked:

"Did I give you eighty million?"
Disciple answered:
The eighty million you gave (really appreciate the gesture), would you say I got it?
You didn't give, and I didn't receive. Stop speaking nonsense. What is important as the actual disciples of Grand Master Lu is practice, practice, practice according to teachings.

✱✱✱

Raising the Brush Swatter

The monk asked: "What is the tenet from the west?"
Zen Master Shunzhi raised his brush swatter.
The monk asked, "This is it. Is it?"
Zen Master Shunzhi put down the brush swatter.
Grand Master Lu asked:
"What is raised? What is put down?"
Disciple's reply:
Raised is oneness and also to deliver sentient beings. Put down is to put down the ego and "I." Did not raise or put down. Only thing left is the eighty million that Grand Master gave! It can never be used up, even if it is used every day.

✱✱✱

Who Should Take the Responsibility?

During the Mahamayuri Ceremony at the True Buddha Temple in Taiwan, Grand Master said that if there is a big earthquake in the future then it would be the responsibility of Master Lianzai. Master Lianzai will be responsible for acquiring wealth and blessings.
Now, Grand Master asked:
"Who would be responsible for respect and subjugation at the Tai-

wan True Buddha Temple?"

Disciple replied:

There is no need to be responsible for anyone. Who is who, who is also who? Respect who, subjugate who?

All is self inflicted. Whoever comes seeking would have to be responsible for themselves.

***

What Is the Meaning of the Word "Thought"?

Reverend Shuangfeng said, "Only thought is high morality."

Zen Master Gu got his directive for enlightenment from the word "thought."

Grand Master Lu asked his disciples:

"How does the word 'thought' become Buddha self nature and enlightenment? What is the real meaning of the word 'thought'?"

Disciple said:

It is not to have thoughts. Non-thought is also not it. No Non-thought is even more not it. Big suspect begets big enlightenment. Little suspect begets small enlightenment. No suspect begets no enlightenment. Who told you, you are hungry? What do you want to eat? You eat what you have. It is like this. Like this! Don't let your imagination run away with you!

***

Number One, First Place

Grand Master Lu's books are number one on the best selling list! Call me number one! If not number one, how else to describe it?

Grand Master Lu asked:

"First place, between you and me, behind closed doors, what's the connection? Do you know?"

Disciple replied:
First place between you and me has no connection. But I have what you have. You know how to wipe your butt behind closed doors and I also know how to wipe myself behind closed doors. Even this minor task has to be done by oneself, so what connection is there?

First place is like throwing away the wiper after you finish wiping yourself. But be sure to wipe clean, so you don't have hemorrhoids!

This conversation is not refined, but to obtain a laughter from Grand Master! You won't ask me to help you wipe yourself?

First place in the time span of the universe has no space or name. Even no first place is still named first place, because its name is first place.

Just to make Grand Master laugh.

***

Origin and Kalpa at the Same Moment

Zen Master Yichu's verse "Beginning and kalpa at the same time," Grand Master Lu asked, "Why is beginning and kalpa at the same time?"

Disciple's reply:
Past, present, and future are three wheels of emptiness. Every moment is continuously changing. Only one will never change.

A rainbow is an example of a moment of continuous change. Is it an image? A rainbow is just rainbow. Ah! How pretty is the rainbow!

Don't mind that there is no trace of forming and no trace of disappearing. Just enjoy the moment.

What is the only thing that won't change? I'll change, I'll change. I'll change, change, change. Change into a cat. Change into a dog. Change back and forth. Still this has not changed. Ah! There is no fun in this game!

Beginning and kalpa? Please, what time is it? Now! I admit, at this time, I confess!

***

What Is Enlightenment?

A monk asked Grand Master, "What is enlightenment?"

Grand Master answered, "Stone buffalo walks on water, a wooden horse flies over mountains at night."

Grand Master Lu asked disciples, "What does this mean?"

Disciple's answer:

Stone and wood are imagination, imagination, imagination! Imagination in your head, unreasonable, but it is still in your head! Invite Grand Master to sit in first class cabin. Very comfortable. Has or has not. Who can tell? Stone buffalo, wooden horse, fly over mountains and forests. The mountains and rivers remain the same. For no reason at all, I pick up a cow dung and kiss a horse's ass.

Thirsty? How about a glass of sugarless lemonade? One taste! Sour.

Disciple: Ah Gui
Paying Homage

Glossary

-A-

Agama (Sanskrit, literally "Sacred Work" or "Scripture")
Four sutras of the Buddhist canon recorded by five hundred of Shakyamuni Buddha's disciples during the First Council which took place immediately after the Buddha's Parinirvana. The four agamas are: The Dirgha Agama, The Madhyama Agama, The Samyukta Agama, and The Ekottara Agama. Some schools consider The Ksudraka Agama (or Ksudraka Pitaka) to be the fifth agama while other schools do not.

Alaya Consciousness (Sanskrit, literally "Abode" or "Dwelling")
One of the Eight Consciousnesses defined in the Yogacara (Consciousness-only) School of Buddhism: (1) eye-consciousness; (2) ear-consciousness; (3) nose-consciousness; (4) tongue-consciousness; (5) body-consciousness; (6) thought-consciousness; (7) manas-consciousness; (8) alaya-consciousness. The alaya-consciousness is usually described as the "seed bed," where all the "seeds" of good and bad karmas are stored, so it is also called "store-house consciousness. This eighth consciousness stores all the actions and experiences from one's lives as karmas. It is unaffected by the death of one's physical body. Hence, karmas follow one from lives to lives exerting influence on the working of seven consciousnesses.

Amitabha Buddha (Sanskrit, literally "Boundless light")
The Buddha of Boundless Light and Longevity, he is one of the Five Wisdom Buddhas and the Lord of the Lotus Family. He embodies the Wisdom of Discerning Awareness which is the antidote to desire and lust. His color is red, element is fire, and direction is west. He

is depicted with his hands forming the meditation mudra. Amitabha Buddha's pure land (paradise) is called Sukhavati and is located in the western direction. He is the Primary Buddha of the Pure Land Sect and often depicted to be accompanied by his two attendants, Avalokitesvara Bodhisattva and Mahasthamaprapta Bodhisattva.

Amitabha Sutra
The sutra as taught by Shakyamuni Buddha which describes the details of Amitabha Buddha and his pureland and what one needs to do to ascend to this pureland.

Amitofo
The Chinese Pin Yin transliteration of "Amitabha Buddha." "Namo Amitofo" (Homage to Amitabha Buddha) is commonly recited in Chinese traditional Buddhism where the name of the buddhas and bodhisattvas are recited. Vajrayana Buddhism traditionally recites the mantras of buddhas and bodhisattvas. For example, the mantra of Amitabha Buddha is "Om ah mee deh wah seh."

Arhat (Sanskrit, literally "Worthy One, Vanquisher of Enemies")
One who has exhausted all defilements and mental afflictions that cause one to take rebirth in the six realms of samsara (the cycle of karma and reincarnation), hence is free from suffering and entered into nirvana (the state of liberation from samsara).

-B-

Bardo Realm
This term refers to a phase between two states. There are six instances of this, as taught by Padmasambhava: (1) bardo between birth and death - our ordinary consciousness during this present lifetime; (2) bardo of the dream state - the state we experience in sleep; (3) bardo

of meditative concentration - the state of meditative stability generally experienced by accomplished meditators; (4) bardo of the moment of death - the state which begins when one begins to die and lasts until the moment when the separation of the mind and body takes place; (5) bardo of reality (Dharmadhatu) - the first phase of the after-death experience; (6) bardo of becoming - the state where the mind moves towards rebirth.

Bodhi
A Sanskrit term used for enlightenment. The term is generally applied to those individuals who have understood the effectiveness of four noble truths and achieved the results of completing the eightfold path. The spiritual condition of a buddha or bodhisattva.

Bodhicitta (Sanskrit, literally "Awakened Mind")
The key to Mahayana Buddhism, it refers both to an enlightened mind and to the resolution arising for the profound compassion to attain an enlightened mind for the purpose of assisting all beings.

Bodhisattva (Sanskrit, literally "Enlightenment-being with Compassion")
One who has developed the altruistic motive of dedicating his existence throughout all rebirths to the attainment of enlightenment in order to liberate other beings who are suffering in samsara (the cycle of karma and reincarnation). In Mahayana Buddhism, there are fifty-two grounds (stages) schemata of enlightenment. It depends on one's merits and virtues, the development of bodhisattva path stands from the forty-first to the fiftieth grounds. Sometimes, it is referring to the "Bodhisattva Path Ten Development Grounds" and they are: (41) Pramudita - joy ground; (42) Vimala - purity ground; (43) Prabhakari - enlightenment ground; (44) Arcismati - wisdom ground; (45) Sudurjaya - no difficulty ground; (46) Abhimukhi - open way ground;

(47) Duramgama - proceeding afar ground; (48) Acala - unperturbed ground; (49) Sadhumati - discriminatory wisdom ground; (50) Dharma megha - dharma cloud ground (see Perfect Enlightenment and Wondrous Enlightenment).

Buddha (Sanskrit, literally "Awakened One")
The term is typically used to refer to the historical Buddha, Shakyamuni Buddha. In Mahayana Buddhism, the term is not restricted to just Shakyamuni Buddha, but may refers to anyone who is enlightened.

Buddha Locana (Buddha Eyes Buddha Mother)
Living Buddha Lian-sheng's lineage comes from Vairocana Buddha, Buddha Locana, and Padmakumara. She is the mother of the Tathagata lineage.

Buddha-nature
The inherent nature of all sentient beings. All sentient beings have the potential to awaken their buddha-nature and become buddhas.

Buddhahood
The stage of enlightenment.

Buddha Land
A spiritual ream of consciousness. Each buddha has their own pure land and one may vow to go to that pure land upon death. When one is reborn in a pure land, one pay proceed on the path of spiritual development until enlightenment is achieved.

-C-

Cause and Effect

A foundational concept Buddhist, Hindu, Jain and Sikh traditions, it is believed that all actions, thoughts and speech generate a result. If one is virtuous in body, speech and mind, then one will have good fortune, harmonious relationships, success, happiness, etc. If one performs non-virtuous deeds of body, speech or mind, one will suffer the consequences. The results of one's deeds, good or bay, will bear fruit in the present life or in future lives. The experiences one currently witnesses are a result of previous actions if past lives, or even from actions committed previously in this current life. Karma, or cause and effect, is what drives the cycle of reincarnation for all sentient beings.

Consciousness

Also translated as mind and discernment, consciousness is the translation of Sanskrit vijnana. Consciousness in this usage does not refer to the mind. Instead it refers to the sensory based perception and the mind. In early schools of Buddhism, they speak of only six consciousnesses: eye (sight) consciousness, ear (hearing) consciousness, nose (smell) consciousness, tongue (taste) consciousness, body (tactile) consciousness, and mind consciousness. These six consciousnesses together shape our understanding of reality. In the Yogacara School, the six consciousnesses were expanded to eight consciousnesses, and later, nine and ten consciousnesses.

Cultivation

The practices one does in order to purify karma, to purify oneself of greed, anger, and ignorance, to create merit, to generate bodhicitta and, ultimately, to achieve enlightenment.

-D-

Daka
Male counterpart of the dakini (see *Dakini*).

Dakini (Sanskrit, literally "Space-goer")
An accomplished female divine being who has attained the clear light and assists Vajrayana practitioners in removing physical hindrances and spiritual obstacles. As they are female beings that travel in space, they are linked with giving birth to the full range of expansive potentialities.

Devadatta
He was a Buddhist monk and a cousin of Shakyamuni Buddha. He was jealous of the Buddha and created a great schism amongst the Sangha (the Buddhist monastic community).

Dharma
Typically, "dharma" is used to describe the body of teachings expounded by the Buddha. However, the word is also used in Buddhist phenomenology as the term for phenomenon, a basic unit of existence and/or experience

Dharma King
A dharma master with a complete knowledge of the Buddhadharma.

Dharma Protectors (Vajra Protector; Wrathful Protector)
An enlightened being that takes on a wrathful form and whose function is to protect Buddhist practitioners.

Dharma Wheel
An eight spoke wheel used as a symbol to represent the teachings of Buddhism. "Turning the dharma wheel" means to teach and spread Buddhist teachings.

Diamond Sutra
An important teaching of Shakyamuni Buddha which shows that all things are ultimately empty and devoid of any inherent reality, including the idea of oneself, other sentient beings, and dharma.

Dragon King
One of the supermundane beings such as a god, asura, gandharvas, and, etc. A dragon king controls the realm of nagas and possesses great wealth.

-E-

Eighteen Fields
The six senses, six sense organs, & six sense consciousness. Any and all experiences are the product of this threefold cause.

Eightfold Path
One of the main teachings of the Buddha that shows the way to attain enlightenment and be free from suffering, the paths are: (1) right view; (2) right intention; (3) right speech; (4) right action; (5) right livelihood; (6) right effort; (7) right mindfulness; (8) right concentration.

Enlightenment
Enlightenment is the translation of the Sanskrit word, Bodhi, which literally means awakened. Enlightenment is awakened to absolute reality as it is.

Evil Planes of Existence
In Buddhism there are six planes of existence, in the wheel of reincarnations. They are the beings in hell (Naraka-gati), hungry ghosts, animals, asura, humans, and deva (Deva-gati)or heavenly beings.

-F-

First Dhyana
First meditation state of four, where the meditator feels joy interest and sense of well-being.

Five Powers
Five attributes obtained by the practice of the five roots - faith, exertion, memory, meditation, and wisdom. Along with the five roots, which are similarly named, they constitute ten of the thirty-seven aids to the way, or the thirty-seven practices leading to enlightenment.

Five Roots
Five kinds of action or cause that are conducive to enlightenment: 1) the root of faith; 2) the root of exertion; 3) the root of memory; 4) the root of meditation; 5) the root of wisdom. The five roots are often listed simply as faith, exertion, memory, meditation, and wisdom. Practice of the five roots gives rise to the five powers, which are similarly named. The five roots and the five powers together constitute ten of the thirty-seven aids to the way, or the thirty-seven practices leading to enlightenment.

-G-

Golden Mother of the Jade Pond
Ruler of all female immortals, she is the most important female deity of the Taoist Pantheon. Known by many names such as Queen Mother of the West, she came into being from the gathering of primordial yin (feminine) energy. Her palace is located on top a peak in the Kunlun Mountain Range. She represents the metal element in the Taoists Five Elements (metal, wood, water, fire, and earth) and there is a Jade Pond near her palace, hence she is also known as the Golden

Mother of Jade Pond.

Guru
Two Sanskrit words – "gu" means darkness and "ru" means light. Therefore, a guru is one who can lead the student from darkness to light – from ignorance to wisdom. In Vajrayana Buddhism, the guru (teacher) is the first and foremost element of one's level of accomplishment. This teacher gives the practitioner the lineage blessing of all past lineage gurus. The guru has also learned, practiced and attained accomplishments in his or her teachings. With the guidance of an authentic guru, one may more quickly reach enlightenment.

Guru Thubten Dargye
Vajra Acharya Thubten Dargye of the Gelug School gave the Highest Yoga Tantra empowerment to Living Buddha Lian-sheng, among many other empowerments.

-H-

-I-

Indra
In Hindu mythology, he is the supreme deity amongst all the deities in the heavens. He governs the thirty-three heavens within the Trayastrimsa Heaven, which is a heavenly realm above the realm of the Four Heavenly Kings, on top of Mount Meru.

-J-

-K-

Ksitigarbha Bodhisattva (Sanskrit, literally "Womb of the Earth")
One of the eight mahasattvas (great beings), the bodhisattva of great vows and like all bodhisattvas, he aspires to deliver sentient beings wandering astray in the six realms (hell denizens, hungry ghosts, animals, asuras, humans, and devas), but he specializes in delivering beings from hell. He is usually represented as a standing venerated figure, holding in his right hand a pilgrim's staff, and in his left a pearl. His famous vow is "Not until the hells are emptied will I become a Buddha; not until all beings are saved will I certify to Bodhi

Kurukulle (Kurukulla Buddha Mother)
She is a Buddha Mother who is the deity of magnetism and harmony. She has a red body and holds a flowery bow and arrow which represent love and desire.

-L-

Lineage Guru
A lineage typically begins with a human being who is able to communicate with the buddhas, learn their teachings and pass the teachings onto a primary disciple. For example: Vajradhara Buddha taught Tilopa,and then these teachings were then passed to Naropa, Marpa, Milarepa and Gampopa successively. Honoring lineage gurus is a vital element of Vajrayana Buddhism and sadhana's typically begin with visualizing the blessing the lineage gurus blessing the practitioner.

-M-

Mahamaudgalyayana
A foremost disciple of Shakyamuni Buddha, who is most accomplished in supernatural powers such as the ability to read minds, transport himself to different realms of existence, speak to spirits,

walk through walls or over water, fly through air and move with the speed of light.

Mahamayuri Vidyarajni
She is the Universal Emanation Body of Tathagata Buddha, the transformation Body of Amitabha Buddha, and the Blissful Body of Sakyamuni Buddha.

Maha Twin Lotus Ponds
This is the Pure Land of the Padmakumara located in the Western Paradise of the Amitabha. By practicing the True Buddha Tantra, one may travel to the Maha Twin Lotus Ponds in meditation or at the time of death.

Mandala (Sanskrit, literally "Circle")
It is a symbol which represents the realms of buddhas, bodhisattvas, or dharma protectors. It also represents various energies of particular enlightened states of mind. It may be in two dimensions, as in a painting, or in three dimensions, such as in the placement of sacred objects. The body or even the world at large may be interpreted as a mandala, as they symbolize various aspects of universal energies. The representations are very artistic with intricate colors and designs to aid in visualization. It also refers to a visualization of an offering multiplying infinitely into the space of the entire universe.

Mantra
Chants used for blessing, invocation of buddhas, offering, harmonization, purification, protection, longevity, etc. It is a sound of sacred syllable, word, or group of words and is the embodying of spiritual power. The chanting of mantra is used as a method of meditation to create spiritual transformation. A mantra also represents the pure speech of enlightened beings, buddhas and bodhisattvas. It is one of the three

secrets of tathagata (pure body, speech, and mind). In Vajrayana Buddhism, the chanting of the mantra (pure speech) is accompanied by visualization (pure mind) and mudra (pure body) as prescribed in sadhana to transform
ordinary body, speech, and mind of a person to the pure body, speech, and mind of a buddha.

Master (Vajra Master; Vajra Acharya)
A master of Vajrayana teachings who has achieved accomplishment in esoteric practices and can guide trainees to overcome spiritual obstacles toward enlightenment. In True Buddha School, the Vajra Master's are identified with yellow collars on their lama robes.

Middle Way (Madhyamaka)
Nagarjuna founded the Middle Way School based on the teachings of emptiness that all things are empty of inherent existence.

-N-

Nirvana (Sanskrit, literally "Cessation")
Cessation of suffering where one is freed from the cycle of rebirth. It is a state where one realizes one's connection with the absolute.

-O-

-P-

Padmakumara (Sanskrit, literally "Lotus Youth")
The sambhogakaya (bliss body) form of Living Buddha Lian-sheng, a great fortune-bestowing and hindrance removing Bodhisattva. For more details about Padmakumara and his abode, the Maha Twin Lotus Ponds in the Western Paradise, see The True Buddha Sutra.

Paramartha-gocara
The third turning of the Dharma Wheel where Buddha's teachings focused on the Buddha-nature and Tathagatagarbha doctrine.

Personal Deity (Yidam)
This is a transcription of Yidam, one of the Three Roots (Guru, Yidam and Dharma Protector) of Vajrayana practitioners. One begins to practice the Yidam Yoga after attaining spiritual responses in the Fourfold Preliminary Practices and the Guru Yoga. In meditation, one merges one's consciousness with a Personal Deity. The Personal Deity represents an enlightened state of consciousness and is chosen to correspond to the basic personality of the practitioner. A True Buddha School practitioner chooses one of the eight major deities (Padmakumara, Amitabha Buddha, Avalokitesvara Bodhisattva, Ksitigarbha Bodhisattva, Maha Cundi Bodhisattva, Yellow Jambhala, Padmasambhava, or Medicine Buddha) as the Yidam and practices the personal deity yoga throughout one's lifetime.

Personal Guardians
See *Dharma Protector*.

Prajna Paramita (Prajna)
The most profound wisdom. It is not the same as knowledge or intelligence, but a more subtle and deeper level of wisdom. This perfect wisdom, or transcendent wisdom, can cross one over from a state of suffering to a state of enlightenment.

Pureland of Ultimate Bliss (Western Pure Land, Sukhavati)
The Pure Land of Amitabha Buddha. A pure land is a place where many Buddhists aspire to be reborn, where they may cultivate diligently until reaching enlightenment, without fear of falling back into the six realms of reincarnation. It is a realm of consciousness rather

than an actual locality.

-Q-

-R-

Ragaraja
Appearing with two heads, as well as the form with a single head, has three eyes, sits on a lotus throne, and has six arms where each arm carries a ritual implement, the most significant being the bow and arrow. When he shoots at the hearts of sentient beings, he brings them love and passion.

Rainbow Temple (Rainbow Villa)
This is the retreat center that Grand Master Lu built in the Cascade Mountains in Western Washington State. As of 2008 it was declared a temple and is now called the "Rainbow Temple."

Reincarnation
In Buddhism, as in Hinduism and various other religions, it is believed that after one dies the spirit enters the bardo realm as it prepares for its next rebirth. One may be reborn in any of the six realms of samsara: hell, heaven, human, animal, asura or hungry ghost. It is also possible for an individual to reincarnate out of samsara and into a pure land, which provides an ideal environment for cultivation and meditation with the intent of reaching enlightenment. An accomplished or realized practitioner (by maintaining conscious awareness during the death process) can choose to return to samsara to continue benefiting sentient beings.

-S-

Sadhana (Sanskrit, literally "A Means of Accomplishing Something")
A means of accomplishment, a sequence of prescribed visualization, mudra, and mantra performed to cut through mental obscuration.

Samadhi (Sanskrit, literally "Make Firm")
It is a non-dualistic state of consciousness where the meditator becomes one with the object of meditation, and there is no separation between the meditator and the object of meditation.

Sariputra
Originally known as Upatisya, he was the son of a Brahman scholar. Before taking refuge in the Buddha, he had already acquired many students of his own, and he eventually led three hundred and fifty students to take refuge in the Buddha. He was renowned for his great wisdom, was the principal disciple of Shakyamuni Buddha, and the person most trusted by the Buddha. He followed the Buddha for more than forty years, during which not one single thought of displeasure or dissatisfaction with the Buddha arose in him. He entered into the tranquil realm of nirvana before the Buddha did.

Seven Factors of Enlightenment
These are:1) mindfulness to remember the dharma; 2) investigation of the dharma; 3) energy; 4) joy or rapture; 4) relaxation or tranquility of both body and mind; 5) concentration a calm, one pointed state; 6) equanimity, to face life with calm of mind, without disturbance, 7) no passion or attachment.

Shakyamuni Buddha
Siddhartha Gautama was born in Lumbini, India (modern day Nepal) sometime between 563 BCE to 483 BCE. He later became known as Shakyamuni Buddha. "Shakya" was his clan name and "muni" means great sage, thus, "the great sage of the Shakya clan." At the age of twen-

ty-nine he left his home, and achieved enlightenment under the Bodhi Tree at age thirty-five. He became the founder of Buddhism and spread the dharma to all beings.

Six Paramitas (Six Perfections of the Bodhisattva Way)
The six perfections or six traits which all spiritual cultivators should perfect. These traits are: (1) generosity; (2) discipline; (3) patience; (4) diligence; (5) meditation; (6) wisdom.

Sixth Patriarch Huineng (638 AD – 713 AD)
A Chinese Zen master who is one of the most important figures in the entire Chinese Buddhist tradition, he is said to have advocated an immediate and direct approach of Buddhist practice to attain enlightenment. In this regard, he is considered the founder of the "Sudden Enlightenment" Southern Zen School of Buddhism.

Six Realms (Six Realms of Samsara)
Comprised of the six realms: (1) devas (gods); (2) asuras; (3) humans; (4) animals; (5) hungry ghosts; (6) beings in hell. Sentient beings are stuck in the six realms until they attain enlightenment, thus freeing them of the need to be reborn in one of these realms.

Six Sense Consciousness (Six Indriyas)
Perceptions and discernments of the six sensory organs (six roots) which shape what we perceive reality to be. The six consciousnesses are: (1) sight-consciousness; (2) hearing-consciousness; (3) scent consciousness; (4) taste-consciousness; (5) body-consciousness; (6) thought-consciousness.

Six Sense Organs
These are: (1) eyes; (2) ears; (3) nose; (4) tongue; (5) body; (6) mind.

Six Senses
These are: (1) sight; (2) sound; (3) smell; (4) taste; (5) touch; (6) consciousness.

Sutra
Meaning "a thread that keeps things together" in Sanskrit which is the metaphor for a set of rules and principles. In Buddhism, sutras are discourses given by the Shakyamuni Buddha. Its usage has broadened to designate discourses by other buddhas such as the Mahavairocana Sutra or other highly regarded sacred Buddhist texts, such as the Platform Sutra.

-T-

Tathagata (Sanskrit, literally "Thus Come One)
A synonym for Buddha. It refers to the primordially pure Buddha-nature which can neither be created anew nor ever destroyed. This nature can remain obscured indefinitely if not purified and developed.

Ten Dharma Realms
Composed of the six realms of samsara, the ten realms are hell denizens, hungry ghosts, animals, asuras, humans, devas, sravakas, pratyekabuddhas, bodhisattvas, and buddhas.

Ten Paramitas
These are: (1) generosity (dana); (2) discipline (sila); (3) patience (ksanti); (4) diligence (virya); (5) meditation (dhyana); (6) wisdom (prajna); (7) expedient means (upaya); (8) vow (pranidhana); (9) power (bala); (10) wisdom-knowledge (jnana).

Ten Virtuous Deeds (Ten Good Deeds)
From The Avatamsaka Sutra; the deeds are abstention from: (1) kill-

ing; (2) stealing; (3) sexual misconduct; (4) divisive speech; (5) harsh speech; (6) lying; (7) irresponsible speech; (8) greed; (9) anger; (10) foolishness.

Three Evil Planes (Three Lower Realms; There Paths Below)
The realms of hell, hungry ghosts and animals.

True Buddha School
In 1975, Living Buddha Lian-sheng established Ling Xian Zong in Taiwan and he officially changed its name to True Buddha School on March 1, 1983. In 1985 Living Buddha Lian-sheng established the main True Buddha School temple, the Ling Shen Ching Tze Temple in Seattle, which was dedicated to the propagation of the True Buddha Tantra.

-U-

-V-

Vairocana Buddha
Also known as the Great Sun Buddha, he is one of the Five Dhyani Buddhas. He typically is depicted as white in color and holds either the Dharmacakra Mudra or the Supreme Wisdom Mudra.

Vajrayana Buddhism (Sanskrit, literally "Diamond Vehicle")
Also known as the Vehicle of Indestructible Reality and Secret Mantrayana ("Mantra Vehicle"), is a form of Mahayana Buddhism in which the guru teaches an accelerated path to enlightenment through the practices of the three secrets of speech (chanting mantras), body (forming mudras), and mind (visualization). There is a
vital element of the teacher-student relationship. The respect of the teacher is extremely vital in Vajrayana because the teacher is the living

embodiment of the Three Jewels of the Buddha, Dharma, and Sangha.

Among its many names, this system is called the secret mantra because the profound three secrets of the buddha (enlightened body, speech, and mind) are taught as the innate nature of all phenomena. However, this profound truth is concealed by the beginningless delusion which has obscured the minds of sentient beings and must be revealed skillfully. It is taught in secret and not shown to practitioners with mundane aspirations. It is called mantra because the three secrets are presented as it actually is which is beyond the perceptions of ordinary mind.

The Vajrayana trainings consist of two phases. In the first phase is the "generation stage." These teachings emphasize on the three secrets of the tathagatas, removing trainee's obscuration to recognize that one's own body, speech, and mind are the same as that of the enlightened body, speech, and mind of a buddha. In the second phase, the "perfection stage," the trainee learns to direct the subtle vital energy and essence within the body's energy channels to manifest great bliss, inner radiance, and emptiness. Through this experiential
sequence, the obscurations of trainee are removed to recognize the innate awareness that has always been there. Through the diligent practice of Vajrayana teachings, one may dissolve the beginningless delusion and attain buddhahood within a single lifetime.

Vimalakirti
A lay Budhisattva introduced in Vimalkirti Sutra teached the meaning of nonduality and expounded on the doctrine of emptiness and the wordless teachings of silence.

-W-

Western Paradise (Western Pure Land, Sukhavati)
The Pure Land of Amitabha Buddha. A pure land is a place where many Buddhists aspire to be reborn, where they may cultivate diligently until reaching enlightenment, without fear of falling back into the six realms of reincarnation. It is a realm of consciousness rather than an actual locality.

-X-

-Y-

-Z-

Zen (Chan) Buddhism
Mahayana Buddhist School that originated in China (called "Chan" in Chinese) that later took root in Japan. It emphasizes the practice of sitting in meditative absorption and de-emphasizes rituals and intellectual studies.

Also From **US Daden Culture**

Sheng-yen Lu Book Collection 51:
Highest Yoga Tantra and Mahamudra
Sale Price: $12.00 USD
ISBN-13: 978-0-9841561-6-0
ISBN-10: 0-9841561-6-X

Sheng-yen Lu Book Collection 148:
The Power of Mantra
Sale Price: $12.00 USD
ISBN-13: 978-0-9841561-1-5
ISBN-10: 0-9841561-1-9

Sheng-yen Lu Book Collection 154:
The Aura of Wisdom
Sale Price: $12.00 USD
ISBN-13: 978-0-9841561-4-6
ISBN-10: 0-9841561-4-3

Sheng-yen Lu Book Collection 163:
Crossing the Ocean of Life and Death
Sale Price: $12.00 USD
ISBN-13: 978-0-9841561-0-0
ISBN-10: 0-9841561-0-0

3440 Foothill Blvd. • Oakland, CA 94601 • U.S.A. • www.usdaden.com

Also From US Daden Culture

Sheng-yen Lu Book Collection 166:
Travel to Worlds Beyond
Sale Price: $12.00 USD
ISBN-13: 978-0-9841561-2-2
ISBN-10: 0-9841561-2-7

Sheng-yen Lu Book Collection 200:
Pages and Pages of Enlightenment
Sale Price: $12.00 USD
ISBN-13: 978-0-9841561-5-3
ISBN-10: 0-9841561-5-1
Ebook ISBN-13: 978-0-9858080-4-4

Sheng-yen Lu Book Collection 202:
Sightings from Thousands of Miles Away
Sale Price: $12.00 USD
ISBN-13: 978-0-9841561-3-9
ISBN-10: 0-9841561-3-5

Sheng-yen Lu Book Collection 223:
Stories of Supreme Spiritual Responses
Sale Price: $12.00 USD
ISBN-13: 978-0-9858080-5-1
ISBN-10: 0985808055

3440 Foothill Blvd. • Oakland, CA 94601 • U.S.A. • www.usdaden.com